# ECCLESIASTES

## and

# SONG OF SOLOMON

## J. Vernon McGee

THOMAS NELSON PUBLISHERS

*Nashville*

Published in Nashville, Tennessee, by Thomas Nelson, Inc., and distributed in Canada by Lawson Falle, Ltd., Cambridge, Ontario.

Scripture quotations are from the KING JAMES VERSION of the Bible.

### Library of Congress Cataloging-in-Publication Data

McGee, J. Vernon (John Vernon), 1904–1988
   [Thru the Bible with J. Vernon McGee]
   Thru the Bible commentary series / J. Vernon McGee.
     p.    cm.
   Reprint. Originally published: Thru the Bible with J. Vernon
McGee. 1975.
   Includes bibliographical references.
   ISBN 0-8407-3272-4
   1. Bible—Commentaries.  I. Title.
BS491.2.M37  1991
220.7′7—dc20
                                   90–41340
                                   CIP

Printed in the United States of America

1 2 3 4 5 6 7 — 96 95 94 93 92 91

# CONTENTS

## ECCLESIASTES

Preface .................................................... v

Introduction .............................................. ix

Outline ................................................... xi

Chapter 1 ................................................. 13

Chapter 2 ................................................. 26

Chapter 3 ................................................. 34

Chapter 4 ................................................. 41

Chapter 5 ................................................. 46

Chapter 6 ................................................. 54

Chapter 7 ................................................. 56

Chapter 8 ................................................. 61

Chapter 9 ................................................. 65

Chapter 10 ................................................ 75

Chapter 11 ................................................ 83

Chapter 12 ................................................ 86

Bibliography .............................................. 96

## SONG OF SOLOMON

Introduction .............................................. 99

Chapter 1 ................................................. 111

Chapter 2 ................................................. 134

Chapter 3 ................................................. 154

Chapter 4 ........................................... 160
Chapter 5 ........................................... 166
Chapter 6 ........................................... 179
Chapters 7 and 8 ................................... 183
Bibliography ....................................... 191

# PREFACE

The radio broadcasts of the Thru the Bible Radio five-year program were transcribed, edited, and published first in single-volume paperbacks to accommodate the radio audience.

There has been a minimal amount of further editing for this publication. Therefore, these messages are not the word-for-word recording of the taped messages which went out over the air. The changes were necessary to accommodate a reading audience rather than a listening audience.

These are popular messages, prepared originally for a radio audience. They should not be considered a commentary on the entire Bible in any sense of that term. These messages are devoid of any attempt to present a theological or technical commentary on the Bible. Behind these messages is a great deal of research and study in order to interpret the Bible from a popular rather than from a scholarly (and too-often boring) viewpoint.

We have definitely and deliberately attempted "to put the cookies on the bottom shelf so that the kiddies could get them."

The fact that these messages have been translated into many languages for radio broadcasting and have been received with enthusiasm reveals the need for a simple teaching of the whole Bible for the masses of the world.

I am indebted to many people and to many sources for bringing this volume into existence. I should express my especial thanks to my secretary, Gertrude Cutler, who supervised the editorial work; to Dr. Elliott R. Cole, my associate, who handled all the detailed work with the publishers; and finally, to my wife Ruth for tenaciously encouraging me from the beginning to put my notes and messages into printed form.

Solomon wrote, ". . . of making many books there is no end; and much study is a weariness of the flesh" (Eccl. 12:12). On a sea of books that flood the marketplace, we launch this series of THRU THE BIBLE with the hope that it might draw many to the one Book, *The Bible.*

J. VERNON McGEE

# ECCLESIASTES

# The Book of
# ECCLESIASTES

## INTRODUCTION

Solomon is the writer. This fact is very well established among conservative expositors, and there is no other reasonable explanation for the book.

Solomon also wrote the Books of Proverbs and the Song of Solomon. We will find Ecclesiastes to be quite different from the Book of Proverbs. In Proverbs we saw the *wisdom* of Solomon; here we shall see the *foolishness* of Solomon. Ecclesiastes is the dramatic autobiography of his life when he was away from God.

*Ecclesiastes* indicates a preacher or a philosopher. I rather like the term philosopher because it is less likely to be misunderstood.

To correctly understand any book of the Bible, it is important to know the purpose for which it was written. We need to back off and get a perspective of the book. We need to put down the telescope on the Word of God before we pick up the microscope. The necessity for this is more evident here than in many of the other books of the Bible.

This is human philosophy apart from God, which must always reach the conclusions that this book reaches. We need to understand this about Ecclesiastes because there are many statements which contradict certain other statements of Scripture.

Actually, it almost frightens us to know that this book has been the favorite of atheists, and they have quoted from it profusely. Voltaire is an example. Today we find the cynic and the critic are apt to quote from this book. And it is quite interesting to note the number of cults that use passages from this book out of context and give them an entirely wrong meaning.

Man has tried to be happy without God; it is being tried every day by millions of people. This book shows the absurdity of the attempt. Solomon was the wisest of men, and he had a wisdom that was God-given. He tried every field of endeavor and pleasure that was known to man, and his conclusion was that all is vanity. The word *vanity* means "empty, purposeless." Satisfaction in life can never be attained in this manner.

God showed Job, a righteous man, that he was a *sinner* in God's sight. In Ecclesiastes God showed Solomon, the wisest man, that he was a *fool* in God's sight. This is a book from which a great many professors, Ph.D.'s and Th.D.s, and preachers could learn a great lesson. In spite of all their wisdom, in spite of all attempts at being intellectual, unregenerate men in the sight of God are fools. That, my friend, is something that is hard to swallow for those who put an emphasis upon their I.Q. and the amount of knowledge and information that they have accumulated.

In Ecclesiastes we learn that without Christ we cannot be satisfied—even if we possess the whole world and all the things that men consider necessary to make their hearts content. The world cannot satisfy the heart because the heart is too large for the object. In the Song of Solomon, we will learn that if we turn from the world and set our affections on Christ, we cannot fathom the infinite preciousness of His love; the Object is too large for the heart.

The key word is *vanity*, which occurs thirty-seven times. The key phrase is "under the sun," which occurs twenty-nine times. Another phrase which recurs is "I said in mine heart." In other words, this book contains the cogitations of man's heart. These are conclusions which men have reached through their own intelligence, their own experiments. Although Solomon's conclusions are not inspired, the Scripture that tells us about them is inspired. This is the reason for the explanatory: "I said in mine heart," "under the sun," and "vanity."

# OUTLINE

I. **Problem Stated: "All Is Vanity," Chapter 1:1–3**

II. **Experiment Made, Chapters 1:4—12:12**
   *(Seeking Satisfaction in the Following:)*
   A. Science, Chapter 1:4–11
   B. Wisdom and Philosophy, Chapter 1:12–18
   C. Pleasure, Chapter 2:1–11
   D. Materialism (Living for the "Now"), Chapter 2:12–26
   E. Fatalism, Chapter 3:1–15
   F. Egotism, Chapters 3:16—4:16
   G. Religion, Chapter 5:1–8
   H. Wealth, Chapters 5:9—6:12
   I. Morality, Chapters 7:1—12:12

III. **Result of Experiment, Chapter 12:13–14**

# CHAPTER 1

The Book of Ecclesiastes is a dramatic autobiography of King Solomon's life when he was away from God. As the Book of Proverbs reveals Solomon's wisdom, the Book of Ecclesiastes reveals his foolishness.

This is not a book without rhyme or reason—not just a bunch of verses stuck together. It begins with the problem stated: All is vanity in this world. Then we will find that experiments are made. Solomon will seek satisfaction through many different avenues, in many different fields. He will try science, the laws of nature, wisdom and philosophy, pleasure and materialism, as well as living for the "now." He will explore fatalism, egotism, religion, wealth, and morality. Then in the final verses of the book he will give us the result of his experiments.

Keep in mind that the conclusions in each experiment are human, not God's truth. This is man under the sun.

Do not misunderstand what is meant by "inspiration" when we say that the Bible is inspired by God. Inspiration guarantees the accuracy of the words of Scripture, not always the *thought* that it expressed. The context should be considered, and attention paid to the person who made the statement and under what circumstances the statement was made. For example, in the betrayal of Christ by Judas, the record of the event is inspired, but the act of Judas was not God-inspired; it was satanic. Also the statements that Solomon makes, while he is searching for satisfaction apart from God, are not always in accord with God's thoughts. Inspiration guarantees that what Solomon *said* has been accurately recorded in Scripture.

## PROBLEM STATED

**The words of the Preacher, the son of David, king in Jerusalem [Eccl. 1:1].**

That description doesn't fit anyone except Solomon, as far as I can tell. David did have other sons, but Solomon was the only one who was king in Jerusalem. He is the philosopher here. We know that he had been given wisdom.

I think that the wisdom God gave Solomon was a little different from what we think it was. We imagine that he was given spiritual insight, but Scripture does not tell us that he even asked for that. He had prayed: "Give therefore thy servant an understanding heart to *judge thy people,* that I may discern between good and bad: for who is able to judge this thy so great a people?" (1 Kings 3:9, italics mine). Apparently God gave him what he asked for: wisdom to rule. He was wise in political economy and probably did a marvelous job of ruling the nation. He brought in an era of peace. Other nations of the world went there to study and to behold the wisdom of Solomon. He gave a testimony for God through the temple with the altar where sacrifice was made for sinners. These were some of the things that the Queen of Sheba learned when she came from the ends of the earth. But in the area of spiritual discernment, Solomon was probably nil.

Now we find Solomon, away from God, launching out with his experiments "under the sun." The man under the sun is a great deal different from the child of God who has been blessed ". . . with all spiritual blessings in heavenly places in Christ" (Eph. 1:3).

**Vanity of vanities, saith the Preacher, vanity of vanities; all is vanity [Eccl. 1:2].**

"Vanity" here speaks of emptiness. It is to waste life without any purpose or any goal. It means to live like an animal or a bird lives. There are a great many people who live like that.

I was in a hotel in the Hawaiian Islands where the jet set come. They fly over the world spending a few days or weeks in Hawaii, then at Acapulco in Mexico, and then the Riviera in France, then to Spain, North Africa, South Africa, and so on. They are world travelers. I watched these folk and listened to their conversation at the dinner table, out in the hotel lobby, and in the elevators. The thing that impressed me about them was how purposeless their lives really are. They talked about people they had seen in other places. They talked about plays they had seen. They would ask, "Where are you going from here?" Someone would say, "Wasn't that place where we went last year a bore!" There was no aim, no goal, no purpose in life. This is also the conclusion of Solomon. Vanity of vanities. Emptiness of emptiness. It is just like a big bag of nothing.

Solomon in the Book of Proverbs gives us gems of wisdom. In Ecclesiastes he gives us globules, not of wisdom, but of folly. Then in the Song of Solomon love is the subject. Wisdom, foolishness, and love—Solomon was an expert in all three fields. He knew how to play the fool; he was wise in government; and his love life was quite a story. Solomon was the wisest of men, but no man ever played the fool more thoroughly than he did. He is the riddle of revelation. He is the paradox of Scripture. The wisest man was the greatest fool. The Book of Ecclesiastes will reveal this.

"Vanity of vanities; all is vanity" is life without God. It is man walking and talking "under the sun," trying to get something out of life.

There is another class of people whom I meet in motels and hotels as I travel. These are the conventioneers. This is the day of conventions. I have listened to them and watched them. They are different from the jet set, but they, too, are looking for something. They have the big cocktail party or beer bust. Then they have a huge banquet with a big show. They try it all, but there is that note of bitterness. There are dregs left in the glass of life.

Now we will find man experimenting. He is going to squeeze the juice of life out of the dry rocks of this mundane existence down here.

**What profit hath a man of all his labour which he taketh under the sun? [Eccl. 1:3].**

Let's keep in mind this is "under the sun"; it is man's viewpoint. God is not giving His viewpoint here.

## EXPERIMENT MADE

His experiments comprise the body of the book, extending from verse 4 through chapter 12, verse 12.

Now the first thing he tries is in the realm of science. He makes a study of the laws of nature. It is interesting that Solomon tried this. Men today still go into the scientific fields of study and spend years, in fact a lifetime, studying these laws of nature. This book is remarkable in giving us these laws of nature.

## SCIENCE

**One generation passeth away, and another generation cometh: but the earth abideth for ever [Eccl. 1:4].**

The earth "abideth for ever" and has a stability that man does not have because man is temporary. Contemporary man is a little different from the man of the past and probably he will be a great deal different from the man of the future, but man is temporary. The continuity of mankind is maintained through births. Most of us were not here a hundred years ago, and we will not be here a hundred years from to-day. In fact, many of us won't be around much longer. However, mankind will continue through succeeding generations. Solomon has noted that: "One generation passeth away, and another generation cometh." Man is a transitory creature. Looking at life in terms of this life only, man is the most colossal failure in God's universe. He has been around only a few years. There are redwood trees in Northern California that were here when Christ was on earth, but they are new-comers compared to rocks around us which geologists tell us have been here millions, maybe billions of years. Although no one knows how long the earth has been here, it was here before man got here, and it will be here after most of us leave. My friend, this adds a certain dimension to life that is rather discouraging and disappointing. Man is not what he thinks he is.

Now we see some very remarkable statements. Here is a revelation that Solomon made a study of the laws of nature and knew a great deal about them. It is quite interesting that these are basic in our day as far as science is concerned.

> **The sun also ariseth, and the sun goeth down, and hasteth to his place where he arose.**
>
> **The wind goeth toward the south, and turneth about unto the north; it whirleth about continually, and the wind returneth again according to his circuits.**
>
> **All the rivers run into the sea; yet the sea is not full; unto the place from whence the rivers come, thither they return again [Eccl. 1:5-7].**

It is very interesting that these accurate observations come from the days of Solomon. Dr. Arthur T. Pierson comments on this fact:

> There is a danger in pressing the words in the Bible into a positive announcement of scientific fact, so marvelous are some of these correspondencies. But it is certainly a curious fact that Solomon should use language entirely consistent with discoveries such as evaporation and storm currents (vv. 6-7). Some have boldly said that Redfield's theory of storms is here explicity stated. Without taking such ground, we ask, who taught Solomon to use terms that readily accommodate facts that the movement of the winds which seem to be so lawless and uncertain, are ruled by laws as positive as those which rule the growth of the plant; and that by evaporation, the waters that fall on the earth are continually rising again, so that the sea never overflows? Ecclesiastes 12:6 is a poetic description of death. How the "silver cord" describes the spinal marrow, the "golden bowl" the basin which holds the brain, the "pitcher" the lungs, and the "wheel" the heart. Without claiming that Solomon was inspired to foretell the circulation of the blood, twenty-six centuries before Harvey announced it, is it not remarkable that the language he uses exactly suits the facts—a wheel pumping up through one pipe to discharge through another?

There are three very interesting statements in verses 5-7.

1. "The sun also ariseth, and the sun goeth down." There is a monotony in nature, but also that which you can depend upon. You can count on the sun coming up and you can depend on it going down—we still use that terminology although we know that the coming up and going down of the sun really is caused by the rotation of the earth. We are standing on a pretty solid piece of earth, and it looks to us as if the sun comes up and the sun goes down. The terminology has accommodated man in all ages. The amazing thing is the precise, regular way that the sun appears and disappears; it is obeying certain laws.

2. "The wind goeth toward the south, and turneth about the north." Today we know that the wind follows certain patterns. Even with our modern gadgets we are not able to predict it well enough to forecast the weather as we would like to. Here in Southern California where we have a monotony of good weather, the weatherman misses the exact prediction about half the time. I have watched this very carefully over the years. The Lord Jesus said, "The wind bloweth where it listeth"—that is, where it wants to blow. It is blowing according to laws. "And thou hearest the sound thereof, but canst not tell whence it cometh, and whither it goeth . . ." (John 3:8)—we can't tell where it is coming from and where it is going. As I am making this study of Ecclesiastes, we have had quite a bit of disturbance across the country. Here in Southern California we never get rain in June or July or August—but we've been having showers! I couldn't believe it when I got in my car the other night and had to use the windshield wipers. The weatherman tells us that there is a low pressure here and a high pressure there. There is movement; winds are blowing. "The wind bloweth where it listeth." Or, as Solomon put it, "The wind goeth toward the south, and turneth about unto the north." At one place the wind is moving north. In Arizona they even had flooding in desert communities, all because of the wind. It is obeying certain laws as it is blowing. How did Solomon know that? He didn't have the gadgets which we have nor the background on which to base his conclusions.

3. "All the rivers run into the sea; yet the sea is not full." Solomon is tacitly speaking of the law of evaporation, of the elevation of mois-

ture into the air. Then the wind comes along, blows that moisture over the land, and it pours out on the earth. The whole process follows certain definite, specific laws. There is nothing haphazard happening, although we may think so. Including verse 4, we have four remarkable statements concerning the laws of nature that make sense and fit right into what men know today. Compare this with other writings that come from one thousand years before Christ. You will find a great deal of false conclusions and superstitions in contrast to the accuracy you find in the Word of God.

Here is another remarkable observation—

**All things are full of labour; man cannot utter it: the eye is not satisfied with seeing, nor the ear filled with hearing [Eccl. 1:8].**

This may not have seemed true before, but since the advent of television it is obvious. Many people watch television for hours day after day. Why? Because the eye is never satisfied with seeing; the ear is never filled with hearing. Most of us love to go to new places and see new scenes. This is one of the enjoyments of life. It is one of the things we can enjoy in this big, wonderful country. I get kidded because I come from Texas, but I must say in all honesty that I have never been in a state that I didn't like. They are all wonderful. We live in a wonderful country and in a wonderful universe.

Man cannot exhaust the exploration of the universe. The more he learns, the more he sees that he should learn. The more he learns, the more he sees how much more there is to learn. This is frustrating. The physical universe is too big for little man. Yet man alone of all God's creatures—as far as we know—is able to comprehend the universe. When a dog bays at the moon, I don't think he knows the distance to the moon, and I don't think he cares. I don't think he recognizes that he lives in a vast universe. I believe that the world of a dog is a very small world. It is no bigger than a bone most of the time. But the eyes and ears of man are never satisfied; he wants to explore.

**The thing that hath been, it is that which shall be; and that which is done is that which shall be done: and there is no new thing under the sun.**

**Is there any thing whereof it may be said, See, this is new? it hath been already of old time, which was before us [Eccl. 1:9-10].**

People think we have come up with something new when we have manufactured a new gadget. I remember what a novelty the telephone was. In West Texas we were on a party line, and when the telephone would ring, you could hear a dozen receivers being taken off the hook. That was the best way to make a public announcement in those days! You say, "Well, television is new, how can it be said that there is nothing new under the sun?" Let me illustrate this.

My grandfather courted my grandmother on an old horsehair sofa in a very staid living room in Mississippi. He proposed to her there. She accepted, and they were married. My dad courted my mother on a train—he met her in a day coach. They traveled by horse and buggy to Tyler, Texas, where they were married. I proposed to my wife down in Texas, as we were sitting in a car. My little grandson may propose to his wife in an airplane or maybe even in a space capsule. You may ask, "Isn't that new?" No, not really. The feeling that my granddad had when his proposal was accepted is the same feeling that I had, and I don't think my little grandson will feel any differently. There is really nothing new under the sun. The environment may change, and there may be new gadgets around, but there really is nothing new under the sun. Man stays the same. Only the stage setting may vary a bit from age to age.

It is said that the atom bomb is new, but the atom has been around for a long time. Actually, the atom is older than man, although man did not know it existed during all that time. All man has accomplished is to make the little atom a very difficult neighbor. The nosy human should have let sleeping dogs lie, but we probe around. Perhaps you are asking, "Well, isn't the computer new?" Not really. God created us with computer brains and electric nervous systems. A mechanical computer brings to man no deep and abiding satisfaction. Man has learned that none of these gadgets contributes anything really new to him.

There is one exception. There is one thing that is new—the New Birth. This is something that comes when you receive Jesus Christ as your Savior. This, my friend, is about the only thing *new* that will come your way.

**There is no remembrance of former things; neither shall there be any remembrance of things that are to come with those that shall come after [Eccl. 1:11].**

Solomon had tried to find satisfaction in the study of science, but he had to come to this conclusion. Man tries to be important. He tries everything in the world to keep himself before the public, but it isn't long until he passes off the stage. "There is no remembrance of former things."

Do you remember who were the popular entertainers of fifty years ago? Do you remember the popular athletes of fifty years ago? Could you name the president of the United States of fifty years ago? Our memories aren't very long. The Scripture says that we spend our time down here as a tale that is told and we can't go back over it again.

You see, this man Solomon is making tremendous experiments, and he is making them in the laboratory of life. He is trying everything that is available to man. In his day and position he was able to go into any field that he chose. Not many men today would be able to do what Solomon did. He first gave himself to the study of the laws of nature, as we have seen, but he found nothing he could learn in nature or in science which was new in the sense that it would bring new life to him.

Solomon's next experimentation will be in the area of wisdom and philosophy.

## WISDOM AND PHILOSOPHY

**I the Preacher was king over Israel in Jerusalem.**

**And I gave my heart to seek and search out by wisdom concerning all things that are done under heaven: this sore travail hath God given to the sons of man to be exercised therewith [Eccl. 1:12-13].**

Solomon spent a lot of time studying the philosophy of the world. He lived nearly a thousand years before Christ, and since we live two thousand years on this side, three thousand years have elapsed. Man has come up with a great deal of gadgetry in that time, but actually man doesn't know any more about philosophy and wisdom than he knew three thousand years ago. There has been no improvement in philosophy and wisdom, neither do they satisfy the heart.

**I have seen all the works that are done under the sun; and, behold, all is vanity and vexation of spirit [Eccl. 1:14].**

All systems of philosophy lead up a blind alley. You can make the same experiment yourself. You can spend your time in studying this subject, and you will find it is actually a waste of time.

We are living in a day when educators are declaring that all the past methods of education were just a waste of time. I wonder how good our present method is. I think that it is also a waste of time. Man can never learn the really important thing—he cannot know God by wisdom and philosophy. His knowledge of God comes *only* through revelation. Philosophy generally leads a person to a pessimistic viewpoint of life.

You cannot take natural man—man who is a lost sinner alienated from God—and give him an education, expecting that education to solve the problems of his life. It will not do that. Philosophy and psychology cannot change human nature, nor can they correct the old nature of man.

**That which is crooked cannot be made straight: and that which is wanting cannot be numbered [Eccl. 1:15].**

"That which is crooked cannot be made straight"—as the twig is bent, the tree inclines. The tree grows crooked because the twig was bent. You and I start out in life with an old nature. We can educate it and do many things to improve it, but, as the Lord Jesus said, "That which is born of the flesh is flesh." It will always be flesh, my friend. That is the reason we must have a new nature—". . . that which is born of the Spirit is spirit" (John 3:6).

For a time we thought that education would solve the problems of life. Now higher education, in fact all education, is coming under the scrutiny of a great many thoughtful people. A committee to study higher education has come up with a novel explanation of our present conditions. They say the rebellion and the general immorality in our schools is taking place because the young people today are more inquiring and more interested in politics and what is happening in their world. I agree that people are more aware of the many terrible things that are happening. The media gather news from the four corners of the earth and broadcast it the same evening. This makes us more aware of what takes place in the world than ever before. There was a time when it took six weeks to complete all the information after an election; so it took that long to find out who had been elected president. Today they can tell you who is going to be elected before they have the election! So I agree with the fact that young people are more aware today. But I heartily disagree with the implication that the things happening on our campuses are actually an *improvement* because the young people are so well informed. There is a deterioration on our campuses. We have come to the day when evil is called good, and good evil. Only an educated man could come up with the conclusion that the deterioration on campuses is not deterioration but actually improvement! If you believe fairy stories, you may want to believe that, but we need to face reality. Education cannot solve the problems of life. Neither can psychology provide the answer. In our day there are clever men and women who have come up with little psychological clichés to explain and solve the problems of life. They coat them with a little Bible, like a bitter pill that is covered with a sugar coating, to make them appear as the biblical solutions. My friend, the Word of God in its entirety contains for the Christians the answers to the problems of life. There are no easy solutions. Studying the Word of God requires a great deal of time and effort and mental "perspiration." Oh, how that is needed among Christians!

Solomon discovered that wisdom and philosophy did not provide the answers to the problems of life.

> **I communed with mine own heart, saying, Lo, I am come to great estate, and have gotten more wisdom than all they that have been before me in Jerusalem: yea, my heart had great experience of wisdom and knowledge [Eccl. 1:16].**

I believe that Solomon was led to a certain amount of arrogance, a certain amount of conceit, since he was wiser than the others. Paul writes that "Knowledge puffeth up . . ." (1 Cor. 8:1). It can inflate an individual like a balloon if he feels that he is a little smarter or better educated than those around him. Remember that education is based on experience, and experience cannot be trusted. Experience must be tested by the Word of God. Unfortunately, many folk today are testing the Word of God by their experience. My friend, if your experience is contrary to the Bible, then it is your experience, not the Word of God, which is wrong.

> **And I gave my heart to know wisdom, and to know madness and folly: I perceived that this also is vexation of spirit [Eccl. 1:17].**

"To know madness and folly"—it is interesting that wisdom and playing the fool are not very far apart. Many smart men in the history of the world have played the fool. Solomon is the notable example of that. King James of England, the one for whom our King James Version of the Bible is named, certainly was not capable of translating. He was called James the fool, because that's what he was, although he thought he was a very smart individual.

Our nation has produced a generation that thinks it is very intelligent and very smart. Yet we cannot even solve the problems that are about us, much less the problems of the world. Solomon gave his heart to know wisdom and also to know madness and folly. He did both.

"I perceived that this also is vexation of spirit." In other words, it was not worth the effort.

**For in much wisdom is much grief: and he that increaseth knowledge increaseth sorrow [Eccl. 1:18].**

Joy and satisfaction do not increase in ratio to the increase of knowledge. Someone has said that when ignorance is bliss, 'tis folly to be wise. There is a certain amount of truth in that. In much wisdom there is much grief. The more we know, the more we increase our problems. Life has become more tedious, has produced more tensions, and all of our scientific gadgets about us are making life almost unbearable. A Christian friend said to me the other day, "I think I will lose my mind if I don't get away from these computers that are controlling life today. The machines that we think are so wonderful and practically worship are drowning us in pollution and driving us to madness." How accurate Solomon was in saying "in much wisdom is much grief," and Solomon did not live in the machine age. He did not see the industrial revolution, but he knew what he was talking about.

# CHAPTER 2

In this chapter we will find Solomon following another course to find satisfaction in life. This is a popular route for modern man who seeks satisfaction in pleasure.

## PLEASURE

**I said in mine heart, Go to now, I will prove thee with mirth, therefore enjoy pleasure: and, behold, this also is vanity [Eccl. 2:1].**

Solomon probably tried everything known in the way of pleasure. We are a sex-mad people. And what do we have to show for it? Well, we certainly have low morals, and we have venereal disease in epidemic proportions. Today the church has entered the field also. I suppose most pastors have a sermon on sex; some of them have a whole series. There are many who feel that the church should have a course to teach our young people about sex. I think that is a tragic mistake. This generation is getting sex right up to their ears—all they need and more. Now Solomon was an expert in the area of sex. He had one thousand wives and concubines, and they were all available to him. A man who had a thousand women around him is some sort of an expert. Solomon tried that way to seek satisfaction. Also he went in for drinking and for entertainment. I suppose he could have put on a performance that would make Las Vegas look like it was penny ante or just a sideshow in a small circus. Solomon went all out for pleasure. "I said in mine heart, Go to now, I will prove thee with mirth, therefore enjoy pleasure." But notice his conclusion: "Behold, this also is vanity"—empty.

**I said of laughter, It is mad: and of mirth, What doeth it? [Eccl. 2:2].**

He probably had a comedian or a court jester to entertain him and tell him the latest jokes—probably many of them questionable. He said, "I found this to be a great waste of time."

> **I sought in mine heart to give myself unto wine, yet acquainting mine heart with wisdom; and to lay hold on folly, till I might see what was that good for the sons of men, which they should do under the heaven all the days of their life [Eccl. 2:3].**

"Under the heaven"—remember that Solomon is a man probing and making experiments apart from God.

> **I made me great works; I builded me houses; I planted me vineyards [Eccl. 2:4].**

These were hobbies with Solomon. Even today the ruins of the stables of Solomon can be seen right in Jerusalem and in several other places. At Megiddo a tourist guide will show you ruins of the troughs where the horses ate. Solomon had stables all over that land, although the Mosaic Law had expressly forbidden a king to multiply horses.

> **I made me gardens and orchards, and I planted trees in them of all kind fruits:**
>
> **I made me pools of water, to water therewith the wood that bringeth forth trees [Eccl. 2:5–6].**

He had irrigation.

> **I got me servants and maidens, and had servants born in my house; also I had great possessions of great and small cattle above all that were in Jerusalem before me [Eccl. 2:7].**

He had a ranch out at the edge of town where he raised cattle. You may be wondering how he could afford all this. Well, Solomon had cornered the gold in his day. He had plenty of spending money, and he built in all the comforts of life.

It is now known that snow was brought down from Mount Hermon so that he could have cold drinks in the summertime. I think Solomon tried everything that a man could try for pleasure. I doubt that modern man could have anything that Solomon did not have.

> **I gathered me also silver and gold, and the peculiar treasure of kings and of the provinces: I gat me men singers and women singers, and the delights of the sons of men, as musical instruments, and that of all sorts [Eccl. 2:8].**

He brought in the best nightclub acts from Las Vegas. He had all kinds of music—from symphony to rock, but it didn't satisfy his heart.

> **So I was great, and increased more than all that were before me in Jerusalem: also my wisdom remained with me.**
>
> **And whatsoever mine eyes desired I kept not from them, I withheld not my heart from any joy; for my heart rejoiced in all my labour: and this was my portion of all my labour [Eccl. 2:9–10].**

Mrs. McGee and I are out in conferences a great deal of the time. In the evenings after a service we need to get away from everyone for a while, and one of the things we like to do is just go walking through a shopping area. I have said to her, "Would you like sometime to be able to buy everything that you see and want?" She answered that she wondered how it would feel to be able to do that. Well, Solomon did just that. Anything his little heart desired, he bought. As he looked out upon this world, there was nothing that it withheld from him.

You would think that all men in that position would be happy.

Well, I don't know why, but they are not. I am told that we have more suicides here in Southern California than the average for the country. One would think it would be the bums on skid row, the down-and-outers, who would be the ones to commit suicide. Life certainly wouldn't seem to be worth much to them. Actually, those are not the ones with the high suicide rate. It is the rich, the famous, the Hollywood movie and television stars, the folk who seem to have made it. They are the ones who commit suicide. Why? They have come to the same conclusion that Solomon did. He had tried everything in the way of pleasure and concluded:

> **Then I looked on all the works that my hands had wrought, and on the labour that I had laboured to do: and, behold, all was vanity and vexation of spirit, and there was no profit under the sun [Eccl. 2:11].**

What a statement from a man who had everything! A great many people will not take Solomon's word for it; they have to make the same experiments—although not to the extent that Solomon did. Eventually they arrive at the same conclusion. They say, "Life is empty." Solomon said, "All was vanity and vexation of spirit, and there was no profit under the sun."

Throughout the remainder of this chapter Solomon moves into another area. I wish I had a better word for it, but I simply call it materialism.

## MATERIALISM

This is living for the *now*, and this should be understood by the people today because we say we are the "now generation." It is a materialistic concept. It is a living for the here and now, living for self, selfishness. Each of these words describes a facet of this type of living.

> **And I turned myself to behold wisdom, and madness, and folly: for what can the man do that cometh after the**

**king? even that which hath been already done [Eccl. 2:12].**

In other words, no one could live it up more than Solomon did. He said they would have to repeat what he had done and would find it very monotonous.

**Then I saw that wisdom excelleth folly, as far as light excelleth darkness [Eccl. 2:13].**

It is better to be a wise man than to be a fool. It is better to be an educated man than to be an ignorant man.

**The wise man's eyes are in his head; but the fool walketh in darkness: and I myself perceived also that one event happeneth to them all [Eccl. 2:14].**

"The wise man's eyes are in his head"—I've heard my parents and my school teachers say to me, "Use your mind. Use your head. Use your eyes." That is what Solomon is saying. A wise man uses his head and his eyes, but "the fool walketh in darkness."

"I myself perceived also that one event happeneth to them all." Regardless of how smart you are, you don't really get too far away from the fool, because you both are going to be carried out feet forward and laid to rest somewhere. You both will end up in the same way.

**Then said I in my heart, As it happeneth to the fool, so it happeneth even to me; and why was I then more wise? Then I said in my heart, that this also is vanity [Eccl. 2:15].**

You would think that a smart fellow would find another way out. "Then I said in my heart, that this also is vanity." It is interesting that modern man with all his tremendous inventions and scientific advances has not been able to extend human life very long. Oh, I know that the average life span has been extended by ten years or more. But put that ten years down by a thousand years, or put it down beside eternity, and what do you have? You don't even have a second on the clock of eternity, my friend. Man really hasn't done very much for himself here on this earth.

> **For there is no remembrance of the wise more than of the fool for ever; seeing that which now is in the days to come shall all be forgotten. And how dieth the wise man? as the fool [Eccl. 2:16].**

They die just the same way.

You may be innately intelligent. You may have a high I.Q. You may have been educated, even have several doctoral degrees, but none of this will help you when it is your time to die. Neither will any of that stop you from dying. When it is your time to go out the door, you will go, and there is nothing in this world that can keep you from it.

> **Therefore I hated life; because the work that is wrought under the sun is grievous unto me: for all is vanity and vexation of spirit [Eccl. 2:17].**

Let me repeat: *Vanity* means that which is empty, meaningless, purposeless. With "all the work that is wrought under the sun" what has been done?

Thomas A. Edison is an example. He worked in a laboratory and developed many things such as the electric light bulb and the Victrola. All of our recording instruments really go back to the work of Edison. He was a genius, but he died just like everyone else. What good did it do him after all?

His laboratory is preserved in Fort Myers, Florida. If you are ever down there, it is worth the time to visit the Edison home and laboratory. He worked in that laboratory day and night. He had insomnia of the worst kind, so he had a little bed in his lab where he would lie down for little naps. He worked day and night, trying out many, many things that never worked out at all. I don't get the impression that life was a thrill for him. I think that Thomas A. Edison found life very boring.

**Yea, I hated all my labour which I had taken under the sun: because I should leave it unto the man that shall be after me [Eccl. 2:18].**

I have to go off and leave all of this someday. Have you ever stopped to think about that? What good is it going to do *you*? Oh, how many folk have worked all their lives to accumulate a little of this world's goods, then they leave it to some godless relative. Some folk intend to leave it to a Christian organization so that their money can propagate the Gospel after they are gone, but have you ever stopped to think how many Christian organizations have become apostate and have departed from teaching the Word of God?

For example, Mr. John Harvard, who founded Harvard University, was a fundamental believer, and he left his money to propagate the fundamental Christian faith. Today you wouldn't find fundamental faith within ten yards of Harvard. They have departed from the faith. The money which Mr. Harvard left has come to be used for the very opposite of what he intended.

People today leave money to so-called Christian organizations, but they have no assurance that the organizations will remain true to the faith.

We know that Solomon faced this same kind of problem, and 1 Kings 12 tells us what happened. He left the kingdom to his son, and it was his son's foolish arrogance that divided the kingdom. What a tragedy that was.

**And who knoweth whether he shall be a wise man or a fool? yet shall he have rule over all my labour wherein I have laboured, and wherein I have shewed myself wise under the sun. This is also vanity [Eccl. 2:19].**

Solomon saw that it was a waste of time to work for something and then to turn it all over to a fool.

> Therefore I went about to cause my heart to despair of
> all the labour which I took under the sun [Eccl. 2:20].

Notice again that this is "under the sun." It is the view of the man apart
from God. This is not the man in Christ seated in the heavenly places
of Ephesians 2:6. This view under the sun always leads to pessimism.

> For all his days are sorrows, and his travail grief; yea,
> his heart taketh not rest in the night. This is also vanity
> [Eccl. 2:23].

Solomon found out that it didn't do any good to worry about it because there was nothing he could do about it.

> There is nothing better for a man, than that he should
> eat and drink, and that he should make his soul enjoy
> good in his labour. This also I saw, that it was from the
> hand of God.

> For who can eat, or who else can hasten hereunto, more
> than I?

> For God giveth to a man that is good in his sight wis-
> dom, and knowledge, and joy: but to the sinner he
> giveth travail, to gather and to heap up, that he may give
> to him that is good before God. This also is vanity and
> vexation of spirit [Eccl. 2:24–26].

If you are living just for self—whether you are God's man or an unregenerate sinner—it will come to naught. It will lead to bitterness in
your heart, and you will be holding nothing but dead leaves in your
hands at the end.

# CHAPTER 3

In this chapter we see that Solomon adopts a certain philosophy of life known as fatalism. This was common among pagans; Buddhism is a fatalistic system; Platonism is fatalism. In our day certain cults give the impression of having a glorious faith in God, but actually the "faith" is fatalism.

The philosophy of fatalism is very popular in modern America. It is my custom to conclude my Bible conferences on Thursday evenings and fly back home on Fridays. On Friday afternoons I board a plane in some distant city and find myself with almost 100 percent male passengers. Who are they? Well, they are married men for the most part who are salesmen or representatives of certain companies. Their families live here in Southern California, and every Friday they get on a plane to come home. Most of them are tired. Their faces show the effect of a week's work. Many of them who are carrying attaché cases will open them up and begin to work out a final report to hand in at the office if they get back in time. Or they will probably put it in the mail when they get home so it will be there for the president of the company to see on Monday. They take their drinks, and after they have their cocktails, they begin to laugh. I can sense that it is the liquor that is laughing. Every now and then, if I sit by one of them and there is an exchange of viewpoints, I find out that they have a fatalistic viewpoint of life.

On one occasion I came home on a plane that passed through some very rough weather. The man next to me looked unconcerned. I said to him, "You didn't seem to be frightened when we went through that bad weather." His response was, "No, there's no use being frightened. What is going to be *will* be. You can't change it. If it's time for your number to come up—there's nothing you can do about it." There he sat, gritting his teeth with a philosophy of life that is very popular. It is called many things, but basically it is fatalism. A great many folk are facing life with that viewpoint.

## FATALISM

Now we find Solomon seeking satisfaction in fatalism.

> To every thing there is a season, and a time to every purpose under the heaven:
>
> A time to be born, and a time to die; a time to plant, and a time to pluck up that which is planted;
>
> A time to kill, and a time to heal; a time to break down, and a time to build up;
>
> A time to weep, and a time to laugh; a time to mourn, and a time to dance;
>
> A time to cast away stones, and a time to gather stones together; a time to embrace, and a time to refrain from embracing;
>
> A time to get, and a time to lose; a time to keep, and a time to cast away;
>
> A time to rend, and a time to sew; a time to keep silence, and a time to speak;
>
> A time to love, and a time to hate; a time of war, and a time of peace [Eccl. 3:1–8].

This is Solomon's viewpoint as he expresses it. In our day we hear the expression, "Take life as it comes."

There is "a time to get, and a time to lose." You played the stock market, and you lost your money. Well, that's the way it was to be.

You were a traveling man away from home, and a certain woman was easy to get, and you invited her up to your room. Your philosophy was that there is "a time to embrace, and a time to refrain from embracing." Taking life as it comes is a philosophy of fatalism.

**What profit hath he that worketh in that wherein he laboureth? [Eccl. 3:9].**

What's the use? Why fight it? If you can't fight them, join them. That is the kind of cliché that is bandied about among men today. This is the way men operate, especially godless men in the business world. Money is made on this kind of basis.

I think that you will find that men who live like this are not filled with joy. They are difficult to live with. I imagine their wives have real problems. They have a cocktail in the evening, and then they become sociable for several hours. After that it is better to stay out of their way.

**I have seen the travail, which God hath given to the sons of men to be exercised in it [Eccl. 3:10].**

Solomon has looked around—"I see people in trouble everywhere; so if I've escaped a little of it, I just consider myself lucky—that's all."

**He hath made every thing beautiful in his time: also he hath set the world in their heart, so that no man can find out the work that God maketh from the beginning to the end [Eccl. 3:11].**

God has allowed men to "set the world in their heart" so they will see that the world does not satisfy—their hearts are still empty. Many men start out with the philosophy that they are going to get all they can out of life. They say, "Life is like an orange, and I'm going to squeeze it for all it's worth." Solomon did that, but it didn't satisfy him at all.

**I know that there is no good in them, but for a man to rejoice, and to do good in his life [Eccl. 3:12].**

There is another group in this crowd: the do-gooders. A man on a plane said to me, "Well, I think a man ought to do good as much as he can. That's what I try to do." Let me tell you that he wasn't doing much good, but that was his philosophy of life.

> **And also that every man should eat and drink, and enjoy the good of all his labour, it is the gift of God [Eccl. 3:13].**

This fellow said, "I see nothing wrong in drinking." And from his point of view, there wasn't anything wrong. This is the fatalism of modern man.

> **I know that, whatsoever God doeth, it shall be for ever: nothing can be put to it, nor any thing taken from it: and God doeth it, that men should fear before him [Eccl. 3:14].**

They talk about God's will as primary, but with this viewpoint a man will say, "If it's not God's will for me to be saved, I won't be saved." You see, fatalism leaves no place for the mercy and grace of God. Fatalism says that God does not hear and answer prayer. My friend, it is God's grace and mercy and love that make life exciting and bring joy into life and give peace to the human heart.

We come to another philosophy at this point, which we call egotism or egoism. It is excessive love of self; an individual's self-interest is the *summum bonum* of life.

## EGOTISM

> **And moreover I saw under the sun the place of judgment, that wickedness was there; and the place of righteousness, that iniquity was there [Eccl. 3:16].**

He is saying that all men are wicked. You can't trust anybody. This is a cynical, although I must confess a rather accurate, viewpoint of the human race.

I was speaking at a conference at which the director said, "Now we want to treat all of you folk who are here as Christian ladies and gentlemen." That was the last thing he should have done because they didn't act like ladies and gentlemen, I assure you.

A friend of mine says that when some men do business, they trust the other individual until he proves himself untrustworthy. He says that he has learned to treat people as crooks until they prove that they are not. Now that is a cynical attitude. Unfortunately, it is reasonably accurate, and I must say that my friend is a successful businessman. He faces the reality as God has said it: ". . . All have sinned . . ." (Rom. 3:23).

Solomon goes on in this vein of thought—

> **I said in mine heart, God shall judge the righteous and the wicked: for there is a time there for every purpose and for every work.**

> **I said in mine heart concerning the estate of the sons of men, that God might manifest them, and that they might see that they themselves are beasts [Eccl. 3:17–18].**

That's not very encouraging!

> **For that which befalleth the sons of men befalleth beasts; even one thing befalleth them: as the one dieth, so dieth the other; yea, they have all one breath; so that a man hath no preeminence above a beast: for all is vanity.**

> **All go unto one place; all are of the dust, and all turn to dust again [Eccl. 3:19–20].**

You recognize, I am sure, that there are several cults which build on this statement. However, we must remember that this is the viewpoint of man under the sun, living for self-interest.

Living for self, enjoying life for self, is the reason men get involved in some projects which are good. For example, many men get interested in athletics and give themselves to it. Others give themselves to art, others to literature, others to music, and many different things. These things are not wrong, but they are selfish; they gratify man's selfish desires.

This viewpoint does not accept the optimist's conclusion. You see, evolution says that man *was* a beast but that he now has become a man. Egoism or egotism or self-interest says that man *is* a beast, which causes the individual to despise others. This philosophy produced the caste system in India and the class system in other parts of the world. It leads to vanity and the feeling of being better than the other man. It has a pessimistic viewpoint of death: man dies as an animal dies. I heard a man say, "Man dies just like a dog dies. When you're dead, you're dead—and that's all there is to it." Since he expects to die like an animal dies, he is going to live for himself in this life and get all he can out of it. This type of teaching is in the contemporary schoolroom. Evolution is a form of it, although it says man *was* a beast, and this says man *is* a beast. It is only a difference of time periods. Both agree that you are going to die like an animal, that you have no soul nor spirit; so you might as well live like an animal.

It is interesting to observe animal behavior with this in mind. I watched a family of little kittens the other day. Believe me, they had no regard for each other. They played together all right, but when food was given to them, they didn't mind pushing one little fellow out. The owner of the cats had to personally feed that little kitten—his brothers and sisters would have been perfectly willing to let him starve to death. Don't they have any compassion? No. Their egoism is their philosophy of life. You see little birds in a nest acting the same way. Each little fellow is taking care of himself. That is the viewpoint of the animal world. The reason man is beginning to react like an animal is because he is being taught in our schools that he *is* an animal.

**Who knoweth the spirit of man that goeth upward, and the spirit of the beast that goeth downward to the earth? [Eccl. 3:21].**

Solomon recognizes that man is different from the beast, for the spirit of man goes upward while the spirit of the beast goes downward—because he is only an animal.

**Wherefore I perceive that there is nothing better, than that a man should rejoice in his own works; for that is his portion: for who shall bring him to see what shall be after him? [Eccl. 3:22].**

In other words, this life is all we are going to get. Again, this is a modern teaching—call it whatever you wish—that the only thing worthwhile is to identify oneself with his environment and live like an animal lives. By the way, this is the ancient version of the "hippie" philosophy which came out of our schools a few years ago.

# CHAPTER 4

This chapter continues the record of Solomon's search for satisfaction through the philosophy of egotism.

> So I returned, and considered all the oppressions that are done under the sun: and behold the tears of such as were oppressed, and they had no comforter; and on the side of their oppressors there was power; but they had no comforter [Eccl. 4:1].

Does this sound to you like any political philosophy in modern America? The egoist rebels against the establishment. He is opposed to it. However, whatever system exists, whoever is ruling, the poor are oppressed. Frankly, the poor always get the bad deal—there is no question about that. They are the ones who are oppressed. So the protest movements begin at this particular juncture.

> Wherefore I praised the dead which are already dead more than the living which are yet alive [Eccl. 4:2].

You have heard the expression: "I wish I were dead." Then, "I'd rather be red than dead" is just reversing it, but both are rebellion against the establishment. Death appears to hold no terror for him whatsoever.

> Yea, better is he than both they, which hath not yet been, who hath not seen the evil work that is done under the sun [Eccl. 4:3].

Here is the other side of the coin: It would be better for future generations if they were never born. "I wish I had never been born" is the way we hear it.

> **Again, I considered all travail, and every right work, that for this a man is envied of his neighbour. This is also vanity and vexation of spirit [Eccl. 4:4].**

It is interesting that the egoist rebels against the establishment, against the oppressor, against that which is wrong, but what about the man who is doing right? What about the man who is trying to do something about it? Well, he says that is no good either. It is a waste of time. This is really a pessimistic view of life!

> **The fool foldeth his hands together, and eateth his own flesh [Eccl. 4:5].**

Does this mean a foolish man is a cannibal? No, it means that he is not willing to do anything to protect himself. He will not work for himself. We have developed quite a society like that today; people want everything given to them.

> **Better is an handful with quietness, than both the hands full with travail and vexation of spirit [Eccl. 4:6].**

Candidly, this is a very good point. Of course this man wants to do "his own thing," but I would say it is better to have it that way than to have the hands full with travail and vexation of spirit.

> **Then I returned, and I saw vanity under the sun [Eccl. 4:7].**

Anyway you go, it is wrong. There is no way out. This is the worst kind of pessimism. No wonder that campuses which major in an egoistic philosophy have the highest incidence of suicide. It is the old sore that has broken out in corruption. Behind all of it is the same pessimism of a philosophy of egoism which teaches that all comes to naught.

> **There is one alone, and there is not a second; yea, he hath neither child nor brother: yet is there no end of all**

his labour; neither is his eye satisfied with riches; neither saith he, For whom do I labour, and bereave my soul of good? This is also vanity, yea, it is a sore travail [Eccl. 4:8].

What a picture this is! Even if you work for somebody else and help them, you are just wasting your time.

Two are better than one; because they have a good reward for their labour [Eccl. 4:9].

Now he is going to give some reasons for teaming up with someone else, but it will be a selfish reason—you may be sure of that. He says that two are better than one "because they have a good reward for their labour." You'll be able to acquire more by teaming up with someone than by trying to do it alone.

For if they fall, the one will lift up his fellow: but woe to him that is alone when he falleth; for he hath not another to help him up [Eccl. 4:10].

Solomon made the discovery that attempting to live just for yourself doesn't mean you can go it alone. You need someone to help you and stand with you. "Woe to him that is alone when he falleth." That is the reason they tell us to team up if we go on a hike rather than going alone. In case of an accident it is well to have someone else around. This is a problem of the many retired folk who live alone. They may fall and break a hip and be unable to get to the telephone. Sometimes it is a day or two before a neighbor looks in on them. So it is better that two be together. If one falls, the other can render help.

Again, if two lie together, then they have heat: but how can one be warm alone? [Eccl. 4:11].

And then one member of a team can give warmth to the other member of the team. I remember as a little boy, I always liked to sleep with my dad in the wintertime because he would warm me up. It was cold. Ours was not a warm house, and we slept in rooms that were unheated. It made quite a difference to sleep with my dad.

**And if one prevail against him, two shall withstand him; and a threefold cord is not quickly broken [Eccl. 4:12].**

If two is company, then three is a crowd, and sometimes it is well to have a crowd, especially if someone is coming against you.

We have problems with crime on our streets today. Often it is the person who is alone who is the victim of crime. I am told that in Washington, D.C., a woman is not permitted to go alone to a public restroom. There must always be another to go along with her. It is tragic that we live in such a day. In spite of what the liberals say, we are in need of law and order in our day. The Bible teaches clearly that unregenerate man has a *sinful* nature. It should be obvious that "civilized" man has not lost his sinful nature and needs restraint rather than liberty. The liberty being exercised in our day is the liberty to hold people up on the street, liberty to mug them, liberty to make obscene calls, liberty to blare out music that only one or two people want to hear, liberty to express oneself in any way. My friend, liberty is not license. You have liberty to swing your fist, but where my nose begins is where your liberty ends. We need to change many of our concepts today.

The self-centered man will not find satisfaction in this life. To be alone in your work may satisfy for a while, but finally you get tired of it. I don't like to travel alone. I go to many conferences in my work, and I take my wife with me everywhere I go. Most of us find that we don't like to go alone.

**Better is a poor and a wise child than an old and foolish king, who will no more be admonished [Eccl. 4:13].**

Solomon was both—a wise child and a very foolish king.

**For out of prison he cometh to reign; whereas also he that is born in his kingdom becometh poor [Eccl. 4:14].**

We should be interested in what happens in federal and state governments because it is going to affect our living. A great many people become poor because the politicians become rich and influential. Certainly folk have a right to protest against that. The corruption that has arisen in our country is wrecking business, making many people poor, and retired folk suffer from it.

**I considered all the living which walk under the sun, with the second child that shall stand up in his stead.**

**There is no end of all the people, even of all that have been before them: they also that come after shall not rejoice in him. Surely this also is vanity and vexation of spirit [Eccl. 4:15–16].**

"The second child that shall stand up in his stead." It is interesting to notice that Solomon was a second child. He was a second child of Bathsheba. He was not the child whom David would have chosen to be the next king. Solomon apparently had noted that since Isaac was not the first child and Jacob was not the first child, God has a way of choosing seconds. If you feel that you are second-class today, remember that you are first-class with God.

The second thing to notice is that later on things seem different from what they were at the time. "They also that come after shall not rejoice in him." Someone, such as a president, may be very popular during his day. Then, as time begins to recede from him, when the glamour boys and publicity men are no longer heard, and the news media are no longer building him up, we can see that his time in office was not a blessing to the nation but actually a time of deterioration. "There is no end of all the people, even of all that have been before them: they also that come after shall not rejoice in him."

# CHAPTER 5

Now Solomon tries something else, and this is something that may interest you a great deal. He tries to find satisfaction in religion, and he does *not* find it. I am going to say several things which may be startling to you, but don't reject them until you think about them just a little.

Did you know that religion has damned more people in this world than anything else has? Take a look at what the pagan religions have done for people in the past and in the present. Look at the condition of India. These people do not have a lower mentality than other peoples of the world. It is their religion that keeps them down. Consider China. As I write, China is in the grip of a terrible dictatorship, but it has made China a nation to be reckoned with. Their pagan religions did not do even that much for them. The Moslem world is fractured and is in sad condition. South America is as rich in natural resources as North America; yet most of the people remain in a miserable condition, and its religion tries to keep it that way. Look at what liberal protestantism and liberal Romanism have done to this country. When this country began to give up its belief in God and its respect for the Bible, when liberalism came into the pulpits of our nation, then deterioration began in our land.

My friend, if you have a religion, I suggest you get rid of it and exchange it for Christ. I personally do not think one can call Christianity a religion. There is no ritual whatsoever given with Christianity. Have you ever stopped to think of that? This is the reason we can have all kinds of churches with different forms of worship—for instance you can sing the Doxology if you want to, but you don't have to. Christianity was never given a form to follow. Why? Because Christianity is a Person. To be a Christian means that you trust Christ. Religion has never been very helpful to man.

## SEEKING SATISFACTION IN RELIGION

Listen to what Solomon is saying now—this is terrific!

**Keep thy foot when thou goest to the house of God, and be more ready to hear, than to give the sacrifice of fools: for they consider not that they do evil [Eccl. 5:1].**

Going to some churches is not only a waste of time; it is *wrong*. It is wrong to give your approval to a liberal pulpit. It is wrong when you do not give your support to a fundamental pastor who is giving out the Word of God. Solomon tried being religious. He went up to the temple, but he warns, "Have as little to do with it as possible; keep your mouth shut. Go and sit, but for goodness' sake don't commit yourself to anything."

**Be not rash with thy mouth, and let not thine heart be hasty to utter any thing before God: for God is in heaven, and thou upon earth: therefore let thy words be few [Eccl. 5:2].**

He is warning, "Do not make any decision under the stress of emotion." Cry at the movies, but don't do it in church. Don't sign a pledge. If you are going to rent an apartment or a house, it's all right to sign for that, but don't commit yourself to God in writing. In other words, make it a religion; go through the form but avoid reality.

My friend, Solomon is not the only one who tried that. There are a lot of unhappy people in our churches today. They never get involved; they just go through a nice sweet little ritual. There is nothing as deadening as that!

**For a dream cometh through the multitude of business; and a fool's voice is known by multitude of words [Eccl. 5:3].**

There are a lot of things being said in church that should not be said.

**When thou vowest a vow unto God, defer not to pay it; for he hath no pleasure in fools: pay that which thou has vowed [Eccl. 5:4].**

Don't go forward at an invitation unless you are really doing business with God. I recall conducting a service after which I was severely criticized because I would not let young people come forward. It was obvious to me that it would have been merely a display. I felt it was better to let them make a decision for Christ right where they were sitting. Oh, how many folk have come forward in a meeting when it has meant nothing to them at all! "When thou vowest a vow unto God, defer not to pay it." Don't break your vow—not to God. You can't promise God things, fail to make good on them, and then expect to maintain a vital relationship with Him.

There is a lot of pious talking and pious promising that is absolutely meaningless because it is never carried out.

Do you know that God actually gave a law concerning vows? Read Leviticus 27. I deal with this chapter in the second volume of my book, *Learning Through Leviticus*. My friend, when you make a vow to God, you had better mean what you say because God is going to hold you to it. There is many a person who is no longer a missionary, many a preacher who is out of the pulpit, many a Christian who has been put on the shelf because they promised God that which they didn't mean at all. It is not a religious ceremony when you are dealing with God. You are dealing with a Person who hears you and expects you to keep your promise.

**Better is it that thou shouldest not vow, than that thou shouldest vow and not pay.**

**Suffer not thy mouth to cause thy flesh to sin; neither say thou before the angel, that it was an error: wherefore should God be angry at the voice, and destroy the work of thine hands? [Eccl. 5:5–6].**

After making a vow to God, we are not to say, "It was an error—I should never have said it; I didn't really mean it." We are dealing with a living God. It seems there are many people who don't know that. As a result, they stand way out on the fringe of the things of God. God is a reality, and we need to be very careful in our dealings with Him.

**For in the multitude of dreams and many words there are also divers vanities: but fear thou God [Eccl. 5:7].**

In "dreams and many words there are also divers vanities"—that is, all kinds of emptiness. They are no substitute for a personal relationship with God. So many people say, "I have had a dream" or "I have had an experience." And they are putting their trust in that. There are many people today who use an experience to test the Word of God. It must be the other way around: All experience must be tested by the Word of God. We are instructed to try the spirits to see whether they are of God or not (see 1 John 4:1). Too many people go out on a tangent of experience and live by that. That is merely religion. That is an appeal to the emotion, an appeal to the aesthetic sense.

My friend, does your faith in Christ rest upon experience, or does it rest upon the naked Word of God? Do you have religion, or do you have Christ?

**If thou seest the oppression of the poor, and violent perverting of judgment and justice in a province, marvel not at the matter: for he that is higher than the highest regardeth; and there be higher than they [Eccl. 5:8].**

In our country we have heard much about corruption in the poverty program. There are so many today who are attempting to get rich at the expense of the poor. God will judge that. "For he that is higher than the highest regardeth." God sees what is going on. I think that any Christian who is in a program in which he sees corruption should get out of the program. If you see corruption in a program, believe me, God sees the corruption in the program, and God will deal with it in judgment.

The history of this world bears that out. God watches what govern-ments do to the poor. Governments that have exploited the poor have fallen. An example is the French Revolution. It wasn't a nice, pretty thing by any means. It was an awful thing. I think it was the judgment of God upon the corruption of a nation in which a few were living at the expense of the many poor.

God has much to say about the relief of the poor. When the Lord Jesus comes to reign during the kingdom age which we call the Mil-lennium, then they will find that there is One reigning who really means business when He says that He is going to do something for the poor. There will be justice and righteousness for them. I don't think that He will put them on any kind of dole system. But each person will make his contribution and will receive justice at His hands.

This brings us to a new section in Solomon's experiments to find satisfaction in life. As we have seen, he tried science, the study of nat-ural laws. He tried wisdom and philosophy, pleasure, and material-ism. He tried living for the "now." He tried fatalism. He tried egoism, living for self. Then, of all things, he tried religion.

Now we will see Solomon engage in another experiment. Solomon was in a position to pursue and enjoy wealth better than anyone else. He was probably the richest man who has ever been on this earth. He gave himself over to the accumulation of gold, and he could buy any-thing that he wanted. The riches of Solomon was the factor that finally brought the downfall of the nation. The greed of the surrounding na-tions was aroused. They wanted to move in to get some of that wealth. God had put up a wall of protection around Israel, but that wall crum-bled, and God allowed the nations to come into Israel and help them-selves.

## SEEKING SATISFACTION IN PURSUIT AND ENJOYMENT OF WEALTH

**He that loveth silver shall not be satisfied with silver; nor he that loveth abundance with increase: this is also vanity [Eccl. 5:10].**

The president of a great corporation comes to the end of the year and sees a tremendous profit, but that actually does not satisfy him. A man may have a big bank account, which offers him some measure of security, but it will not really satisfy him. Wealth will not bring satisfaction in life.

Wealth is not wrong in itself. The Scripture never condemns wealth. It condemns the *love* of money. Not the money itself, but the *love* of money is a root of all evil (see 1 Tim. 6:10). To accumulate wealth for wealth's sake is wrong. The miser thinks dollars are flat so they can be stacked; the spendthrift thinks they are round so they can be rolled. Both are entirely wrong.

Man's attitude toward money is the issue. There is nothing wrong with our profit system itself. The wrong is in the people who are in it. It is the love of money which is wrong. The love of money makes people try to get rich for riches' sake.

We see men who are held together, bound together in an arrangement just to make money for money's sake. I was interested in hearing a comedian tell about a play he had a part in producing. He was thanking all those who had participated and was telling how they had all cooperated. It was a very lovely speech with no trace of humor in it. When he got to the end, he said, "And we have all been held together in this endeavor by one thing"—he paused a moment—"greed!" Yes, greed was the ingredient that held them together to make the production. That is the ingredient that holds big business together. It holds the Mafia together. It holds a great many organizations together.

I must confess that I believe it is wrong for one man or one organization to accumulate so much money when others are in poverty and need. This may sound radical, but I do believe that eventually something must be done about that. Look at India for an example. The maharaja has become immensely wealthy while the masses are poverty-stricken. God condemns that kind of thing. He condemns it because of the love of money and the use which is made of it. In our own country greed is the thing that is wrong with godless capitalism and godless labor. Greed—the love of money. It would be so wonderful if man would *make* money for the glory of God. It would be wonderful if man *labored* for money for the glory of God. It would be so wonderful if money were put to its proper use. The only cure for greed, of course, is to have Christ in the heart!

> **When goods increase, they are increased that eat them: and what good is there to the owners thereof, saving the beholding of them with their eyes? [Eccl. 5:11].**

Growth just for the sake of growth is no good at all. This is true of a business or even of a Christian organization or church. I have learned it by personal experience.

For years I was the pastor of a large church. Just to grow for the sake of growing so one can have a big church is nothing in the world but a big headache. There is no fun in it. There is no joy in it. The Lord taught me that to grow for the glory of God is to be my one purpose in life. I keep this goal before me: Vernon McGee, you do this one thing, get out the Word of God.

> **The sleep of a labouring man is sweet, whether he eat little or much: but the abundance of the rich will not suffer him to sleep [Eccl. 5:12].**

The laboring man may not have too much to eat. That keeps him from being a glutton, and he probably sleeps a lot better by not overeating. The rich man has an abundance. In fact, he has gourmet food all the time, and he gets pretty tired of it. He loses his appetite for it. Besides that, he has to worry about his riches, which keeps him awake at night. When we were in Hawaii with one of our tours, we were permitted to stay in a lovely hotel because of the size of our tour. I noticed how unhappy the people in the hotel seemed to be. They were people who had come to Hawaii to have a good time, but they were always worrying about their things. One woman spent thirty minutes getting her jewels in a safe-deposit box. When I got to the desk, the girl said, "She's been here before and she'll be back a dozen times to check on them or take out a piece to wear and bring it back again." You know, I was glad my wife didn't have that kind of problem. That rich woman had a real problem—probably one hundred thousand dollars worth of jewels to worry about. Riches multiply anxieties. Maybe that is one reason the Lord didn't let me become rich!

**There is a sore evil which I have seen under the sun, namely, riches kept for the owners thereof to their hurt [Eccl. 5:13].**

Riches actually hurt rather than help a great many people. Sometimes the poor man is happier than the rich man. However, the apostle Paul said that he knew both how to abound and how to be abased (see Phil. 4:12). Frankly, I'd like to try both.

**But those riches perish by evil travail: and he begetteth a son, and there is nothing in his hand [Eccl. 5:14].**

He is saying that a man can accumulate a fortune and leave it to a son, and the boy will run through it—he will spend it all. Today men have become pretty wise about that. A man doesn't leave the money to his son directly, but in a trusteeship so that someone else doles out the money to the boy in small amounts to preserve the family fortune.

There are a lot of prominent men today who never made a dime in their lives. The reason they are rich is because they inherited it. They lack discernment in the use of the money; yet they are in positions of influence. This is one of our problems today.

I think that eventually there will be a division in our nation which will not be between races, but will narrow down to the rich and the poor. That has always been the line of demarcation. I believe many rich people sense this, which explains why so many of the wealthy are politically liberal in their thinking. They already have their money, and no one can touch it; so they are willing to bring in liberal programs which will be supported by the taxes that you and I pay. The wealthy do not pay for those programs. That is a real problem. Solomon understood and spoke into that kind of situation. Solomon learned that wealth does not satisfy, nor is it the solution to the problems of life.

# CHAPTER 6

This chapter concludes Solomon's pursuit and enjoyment of wealth in his search for satisfaction.

> There is an evil which I have seen under the sun, and it is common among men:
>
> A man to whom God hath given riches, wealth, and honour, so that he wanteth nothing for his soul of all that he desireth, yet God giveth him not power to eat thereof, but a stranger eateth it: this is vanity, and it is an evil disease [Eccl. 6:1-2].

A friend told me that when he was in a hotel in Florida, he saw John D. Rockefeller, Sr., sitting and eating his meal. He had just a few little crumbs, some health food, that had been set before him. Over at a side table my friend saw one of the men who worked as a waiter in the hotel sitting with a big juicy steak in front of him. The man who could afford the steak couldn't eat one; the man who could not afford the steak had one to eat because he worked for the hotel. It is better to have a good appetite than a big bank account!

> If a man beget an hundred children, and live many years, so that the days of his years be many, and his soul be not filled with good, and also that he have no burial; I say, that an untimely birth is better than he [Eccl. 6:3].

The rich man can eat only three meals a day, he can sleep on only one bed at a time, and he cannot live longer than the poor man—no matter how many doctors he may have—and he takes nothing with him when he leaves. There is no pocket in a shroud. Job was a rich man, and he said that he had come here with nothing and he was going out the same way. It is rather empty to give one's life to the pursuit of that which does not bring happiness here and has no value hereafter. Some people spend their lives in this kind of an emptiness.

# CHAPTER 7

This is the last experiment that Solomon tries. He has made experiments in everything under the sun to see if any of it would bring satisfaction and enjoyment to him. He tried science, the study of the natural laws of the universe, which made some contribution but did not satisfy him. Then he went into the study of philosophy and psychology. They didn't satisfy. He went the limit on pleasure and materialism. He tried fatalism, which is such a popular philosophy of life today. He tried egoism, living for self. Then he tried religion—no religion can satisfy because only Christ can satisfy the heart. Wealth was another thing which Solomon tried. He was the wealthiest man in the world, but he found that wealth did not bring satisfaction in and of itself.

Now we will see him try the last experiment: morality. Today we would call him a "do-gooder." I would say that this is the place to which the majority of the people in America are moving. (I think the majority would still be classified as do-gooders.) They are going down the middle of the road on the freeway of life. This group can be described as the Babbitts, doing business in the Big City, under a neon sign, living out in suburbia, in a sedate, secluded, exclusive neighborhood, and taking it easy. Their children go to the best schools. They move with the best crowds. They go to the best church, the richest church in the neighborhood, the one with the tallest steeple, the loudest chimes, and the most educated preacher, who knows everything that man can possibly know, except the Bible (of course, if he did know and preach the Bible, he would lose his job). This is the kind of do-good society Solomon now tries.

## SEEKING SATISFACTION IN MORALITY
## THE GOOD LIFE

**A good name is better than precious ointment; and the day of death than the day of one's birth [Eccl. 7:1].**

That is true, by the way. There is nothing wrong with that statement. A good name *is* better than precious ointment. It is gratifying to a man to have people say he is a wonderful neighbor and that they have never had an argument with him, that he won't discuss religion or politics, or won't get involved in any kind of bad situation. He just smiles and goes right down the middle of the road, never veering to the right or to the left. He is a respectable person, recognized in the community. He joins different organizations of the town and does business with all kinds of people. Some day at his funeral the preacher will say all kinds of good things about him to try to push him into heaven. Solomon says a good reputation and a long eulogy at your funeral are what we should strive for down here. But will that satisfy the heart?

**It is better to go to the house of mourning, than to go to the house of feasting: for that is the end of all men; and the living will lay it to his heart [Eccl. 7:2].**

All of this life of morality and do-goodism is done in a dignified manner. People go to a club meeting and listen to a man come and talk about pollution. They don't *do* anything about it, but they sit and talk about it in a very dignified way. The next week someone talks to them on civic problems. They sit and listen to that, and again nothing will be done. Then they all go to the funeral of one of the men in their fraternal lodge and hear nice things said about him. Nobody is particularly moved; no one will miss him too much. This is just how life is in our hometown.

That kind of life cannot satisfy the needs of man. To me, that life would be *blah*. I am glad I have never lived like that, and I don't live like that today. It is not really *living*. I think this is the worst situation of them all. Frankly, I cannot blame a lot of young people who are rebelling against that kind of society.

**Sorrow is better than laughter: for by the sadness of the countenance the heart is made better [Eccl. 7:3].**

People today do anything to avoid sorrow. We have it arranged now so that you can laugh all the way to the cemetery. Reality is so covered over with flowers and soft music and a preacher saying a lot of easy things, nice things, that everyone goes home and says, "My, that was a nice funeral"—and forgets the grim reality of death as soon as possible.

**The heart of the wise is in the house of mourning; but the heart of fools is in the house of mirth [Eccl. 7:4].**

They don't get more than fifty yards from the cemetery until someone tells a joke and they all have a good laugh. This is living in the presence of death. Somehow it doesn't occur to these folk, as they see their friends slipping out of this life, that they, too, are moving along to death. Doesn't it occur to them that it might be well for them to check to see where they are going? Are they saved? Are they lost? Are they rightly related to God? They don't consider that important. They give to the Community Chest and are active in Red Cross. They are involved citizens in the community. They wouldn't dare confess Christ and take a public stand for Him.

**It is better to hear the rebuke of the wise, than for a man to hear the song of fools.**

**For as the crackling of thorns under a pot, so is the laughter of the fool: this also is vanity [Eccl. 7:5–6].**

Solomon's point is this: Why not try both groups? Listen to the rebuke of a wise person, then go down and listen to a rock band and enjoy that also. One may be better than the other, but it is easier to go with both groups. This is the picture through the remainder of this chapter.

**Be not hasty in thy spirit to be angry: for anger resteth in the bosom of fools [Eccl. 7:9].**

Don't get angry at anything. Be a nice fellow, stay friends with everyone because that will help business. Go the easy way, walk softly. Don't be an extremist, be willing to compromise. Go with one crowd to be popular with them, and the next night go with a different crowd to be popular with them. You see, the do-gooder in this chapter is the man who lives like hell on Saturday night and then goes to church and passes for a Christian on Sunday. A man who had been stone drunk on Saturday night saw me on Sunday morning and said, "I want you to know that I am a Christian. What do you think I am, a pagan?" And that's what he was, a pagan.

**Wisdom is good with an inheritance: and by it there is profit to them that see the sun [Eccl. 7:11].**

In the Book of Proverbs we see that "wisdom" is another name for Christ. Christ has been made unto us wisdom. Oh, how this do-gooder needs to have Christ!

**For wisdom is a defence, and money is a defence: but the excellency of knowledge is, that wisdom giveth life to them that have it [Eccl. 7:12].**

"Money is a defence"—this man wants plenty of money, but he doesn't want Christ.

"Wisdom giveth life to them that have it." And you can't buy life with money. Medical science may be able to extend your life for a few years, but it doesn't give eternal life here and out yonder in eternity. Only wisdom, which is Christ, can do that.

**Also take no heed unto all words that are spoken; lest
thou hear thy servant curse thee [Eccl. 7:21].**

Don't be disturbed by reports that somebody who knows you well says
you are a crook. If you take the middle of the road, in the long run the
community will applaud you.

My friend, seeking satisfaction in life by just trying to be a do-
gooder is living like a vegetable, not a man! Yet this is the lifestyle of
the majority in modern America. They will go to the burlesque show
on Saturday night and to church on Sunday morning! What hypocrisy!
We have seen our youth rebelling against this type of living. There are
two thousand of them over on the island of Hawaii. I had the privilege
of ministering to some of them, and quite a few turned to Christ. They
have tried everything else. But why didn't they find Christ in their
homes in which their parents were church members? They saw that
there was something radically missing in their homes and in their
churches. They have seen the hypocrisy, the emptiness of the life of
the moralist, the do-gooder.

I believe it is easier to reach a godless atheist than a hypocritical
churchgoer. The godless atheist may respond when he hears the Gospel for the first time, but the hypocritical churchgoer has heard the
Gospel again and again and has become hardened to it. That is the real
tragedy.

# CHAPTER 8

This chapter continues with the man who is lukewarm. He blows neither hot nor cold. The moralists and the do-gooders say that they are living by the Golden Rule, but they don't seem to have any idea of what the Golden Rule is and what it requires. Solomon observes that there doesn't seem to be much difference between the wicked and the righteous.

> Who is as the wise man? and who knoweth the interpretation of a thing? a man's wisdom maketh his face to shine, and the boldness of his face shall be changed [Eccl. 8:1].

Only Christ who is real wisdom can change a man's life. He can come into a life and bring excitement, joy, and peace. He can give us all the things that are needed today to deliver us from living a mediocre existence.

> I counsel thee to keep the king's commandment, and that in regard of the oath of God.
>
> Be not hasty to go out of his sight: stand not in an evil thing; for he doeth whatsoever pleaseth him [Eccl. 8:2-3].

He is saying, "Be careful what you do. Don't get into trouble."

> Where the word of a king is, there is power: and who may say unto him, What doest thou? [Eccl. 8:4].

Now the king can take a stand for what he believes because he has the liberty to do so. My friend, why don't you live like a king and take a stand for Christ?

I talked to a young vagrant who had adopted what was then called the hippie life style. I asked him, "Why in the world do you take up this life style? Why are you dressed like you are?" He said, "Man, I want liberty; I want freedom. I want to live as I please." I said, "Let me ask you this one question: If you changed your garb and went back to your crowd, would they accept you?" He thought a moment and then said, "I guess they wouldn't." So I asked, "Then you don't have much liberty, do you?"

Young people feel that they *must* have the approval of the crowd, of the pack, so they really don't know what liberty is. A great many of them take drugs for no other reason than to be accepted by the crowd. I asked the young man, "Do you think that I don't have freedom because I dress as I dress?" He answered, "Yes, I would say that." Then I told him that I have a freedom which he didn't have. I told him that I don't dress like this all the time. I can dress any way that I please—and I do. I don't conform to a pattern. I have liberty. I said, "You and I are living in a world where there is rebellion against God—that is the direction mankind is moving. But I can bow my knee to the Lord Jesus Christ. I can call Him my Lord and my Savior. That is *real* freedom. I am not going in the direction of the crowd. I have made my choice. Young man, if you want real freedom, come to Christ. Jesus said, 'If the Son therefore shall make you free, ye shall be free indeed'" (John 8:36). That is freedom.

It is hard for people to understand that the do-gooder is just as much in rebellion against God as the criminal in the jail and that he is bound as securely by the rules of his group and the patterns they set. He is bound to a life style that goes down the middle of the road.

**There is no man that hath power over the spirit to retain the spirit; neither hath he power in the day of death: and there is no discharge in that war; neither shall wickedness deliver those that are given to it [Eccl. 8:8].**

If he continues taking that cocktail to conform to the group he associates with, one of these days he is going to be an alcoholic. (Oh, there are millions of them in our country, and they are all do-gooders!) And finally death will come to him—"neither hath he power in the day of death."

**Because sentence against an evil work is not executed speedily, therefore the heart of the sons of men is fully set in them to do evil [Eccl. 8:11].**

What a picture of that which is happening in our contemporary society! When judgment is not executed, men do more and more evil work because evil is in the hearts of men. Even men who call themselves Christian continue in sin, saying, "Look, I've been in sin for five years, and God has done nothing about it!" Well, that already reveals His judgment upon you. He has done nothing about it because He is way down the road waiting for you. In fact, He can wait until eternity—you can't. ". . . Behold, now is the accepted time; behold, now is the day of salvation" (2 Cor. 6:2). God grants you *today* so that you can turn to Him.

**There is a vanity which is done upon the earth; that there be just men, unto whom it happeneth according to the work of the wicked; again, there be wicked men, to whom it happeneth according to the work of the righteous: I said that this also is vanity [Eccl. 8:14].**

Solomon observes that when you look at the surface of things, there does not seem to be too much difference between the wicked and the righteous. It seems that it really doesn't make any difference whether one is wicked or righteous because both come to the same end.

**Then I commended mirth, because a man hath no better thing under the sun, than to eat, and to drink, and to be merry: for that shall abide with him of his labour the**

**days of his life, which God giveth him under the sun [Eccl. 8:15].**

"Eat, . . . drink, and . . . be merry"—he concludes that the best thing to do is to enjoy life and to enjoy the labor "which God giveth him under the sun." That is the most empty philosophy of life that anyone can have.

# CHAPTER 9

We have labeled the moralist as the do-gooder. This is where we see him in action. We have seen that this is the man who says, "I believe that if you pay your honest debts and live a good life, God will accept you." He is like the average American who travels down the middle of the road on the freeway of life. He is Babbitt on Main Street in Big City, doing business under a neon sign but living in the sedate, secluded, and exclusive neighborhood in the suburbs. He is the one who feels that he is going to heaven on his own propulsion. "I am working out my own salvation, and I'm really a pretty good fellow after all." He has a hard philosophy of life and very little real joy. Oh, he has his "happy hour" each evening when he has his cocktail, but he comes to some very doleful and pessimistic conclusions.

We have seen that many of the teachings of the Book of Ecclesiastes are quite radical. They present the philosophy of man *under the sun*. They do not present the Christian viewpoint, nor do they represent God's viewpoint. They tell us the inevitable conclusions that are reached by the man under the sun. I find it a doleful book, and I find this chapter especially so. This book of the Bible is like a black sheep in a flock of sheep. One can take many passages out of this book which seem to contradict the other portions of Scripture. They express ideas that are contrary to some of the great teachings of Scripture, which explains why this book has been a favorite among atheists. Volney and Voltaire quoted from it frequently. It fosters a pessimistic philosophy of life like Schopenhauer had. Some of the modern cults predicate the main thesis of their systems on this book.

How did this book get into the canon of Scripture? Well, it is obvious that one must go back to the purpose of the author. What is his thesis? What is he demonstrating? Is he trying to set forth Christian principles? We must always remember that Solomon is speaking of life apart from God. He has tried to make an experiment to see how to be happy without God. These are the conclusions that he has come to "under the sun." This is the way the man of the world looks at life. So then it is no surprise that unbelievers would quote from this book.

Let me give you an illustration to help you understand this book. Halfway between high tide and low tide is what they call the *mean* tide, which is sea level. There is a realm of life below sea level; there is a realm of life above sea level. Actually, they are like two different worlds. In the world below sea level there are certain chemical elements in a world that is aqueous. Above the sea level there are different combinations of chemical elements in a world that is gaseous. Below sea level are the fish with fins. Above are the birds with wings. There are two ways of life. The mockingbird does not tell the tuna fish that he is all wrong because he doesn't have feathers. The monkey and the barracuda could actually have a big debate on which direction is sea level. The monkey would say that sea level is down; the barracuda would argue that sea level is up.

Now Ecclesiastes is "under the sun." The Christian life is in the heavenly places where God is. Man under the sun will have a different view of life from the view of God who is above the sun. We are looking at two different worlds, two different ways of life. Life *under* the sun is a mundane existence apart from God. It views a future and an eternity without God. The Christian life is a contrast to this in every way because man has been saved by the grace of God and is a display of His grace.

So there are two different spheres, and the laws and principles of one will not apply to the other. They are as far apart as that which is below sea level and that which is above sea level. Because this is true, it is a waste of time to tell the non-Christian, "If ye then be risen with Christ, seek those things which are above, where Christ sitteth on the right hand of God" (Col. 3:1). That man is not even in Christ; he is not risen with Christ. Therefore he *cannot* seek those things which are above. He first needs to be born again, to become a new creature. You see, it is no use talking to a non-Christian as if he were a man in Christ because he isn't. It would be like trying to teach a mud turtle to fly. The mud turtle likes the mud; he is not even interested in flying.

As we have seen, Ecclesiastes is the record of experiments that Solomon made with life. He tried everything "under the sun" to see if he could find satisfaction for his soul. Everything must be interpreted in that light.

Solomon tried the pursuit of knowledge and came to the conclusion, ". . . of making many books there is no end" (Eccl. 12:12). He tried pleasure and the outcome was, "I hated life." He tried riches and came to the conclusion, "He that loveth silver shall not be satisfied with silver" (Eccl. 5:10). Then he tried religion and concluded that it will make one become a lunatic or a racketeer, a crank or a crook, a nut or a bum. Then he tried fame and a good name; he tried morality. All he could say was that it was all vanity and vexation of spirit.

Thackeray wrote a wonderful novel called *Vanity Fair*. It is the story of a girl named Becky, and it is set in the time of the wars of Napoleon. It tells of the littleness and of the sin in the lives of the characters as they lived their lives apart from God (Thackeray was a Christian). He concluded the book by saying, "The play is over. We put the puppets back in the box. All is vanity and vexation of spirit."

By the way, you could do the same thing with the entertainment and pleasure capitals of our country. They are places of fame and riches and also places that have a monopoly on sleeping pills and narcotics. Life is empty without God and without Christ.

Augustine gave us that often-quoted expression, "Thou has made us for Thyself, and the heart of man is restless until it finds its rest in Thee" (Confessions, Bk. 1, Sec. 1). The human heart is so constructed that you could put the whole world in it and still it would not be filled.

Quotations from Ecclesiastes have been used to support socialism. There is only one answer for statism or regimentation. Christ is the answer, the only answer. All other routes lead to emptiness and frustration. With Him there is life abundant.

**For all this I considered in my heart even to declare all this, that the righteous, and the wise, and their works, are in the hand of God: no man knoweth either love or hatred by all that is before them [Eccl. 9:1].**

He is not worried about the future. Eternity is a realm he doesn't even think about because he knows nothing about it.

> **All things come alike to all: there is one event to the righteous, and to the wicked; to the good and to the clean, and to the unclean; to him that sacrificeth, and to him that sacrificeth not: as is the good, so is the sinner; and he that sweareth, as he that feareth an oath [Eccl. 9:2].**

It looks to him as if it doesn't make any difference which direction you go. They all come out the same way anyhow. Remember, this is not God's answer. This is the way it looks to man under the sun as he observes the lives of people around him.

> **This is an evil among all things that are done under the sun, that there is one event unto all: yea, also the heart of the sons of men is full of evil, and madness is in their heart while they live, and after that they go to the dead [Eccl. 9:3].**

Why should anyone work at all? Life is just a big lottery, and you are the victim of your circumstances. The fellow who was lucky enough to get his share of it, ought to share it with you. The philosophies of our day are not saying anything new. Karl Marx didn't say anything new— Solomon was way ahead of him.

> **For to him that is joined to all the living there is hope: for a living dog is better than a dead lion [Eccl. 9:4].**

If you follow along this basic premise, it is eat, drink, and be merry for tomorrow you die. Then, whether you are a fool or a wise man doesn't make much difference. It's still better to be alive than dead even if you are a fool while you are alive—"for a living dog is better than a dead lion."

**For the living know that they shall die: but the dead
know not any thing, neither have they any more a reward; for the memory of them is forgotten [Eccl. 8:5].**

This is where the idea of a "soul sleep" arises (see also v. 10). All of
this is the observation of the man under the sun. This is the way it
looks if death is the end and there is nothing after death. That is why
he says it would be better to be a living dog than a dead lion.

God has told us what happens after death. The body is put into the
grave, and it is the *body* that sleeps in the grave. Scripture makes it
very clear that the soul of the child of God goes to be with the Lord:
"Therefore we are always confident, knowing that, whilst we are at
home in the body, we are absent form the Lord: (For we walk by faith,
not by sight:) We are confident, I say, and willing rather to be absent
from the body, and to be present with the Lord" (2 Cor. 5:6–8). The
soul, the real person, goes to be with the Lord—absent from the body,
present with the Lord. The bodies you and I are living in are only our
earthly tabernacles or tents, and we'll move out of them someday. So
you see, soul sleep is not even a Christian viewpoint.

**Also their love, and their hatred, and their envy, is now
perished; neither have they any more a portion for ever
in any thing that is done under the sun [Eccl. 9:6].**

I told you that this is a doleful chapter. It looks as if life is futile, purposeless, and without meaning. If death is the end of everything, then
man is just like an animal. The evolutionist says that man once was an
animal, and this man under the sun says man is like an animal now.
The end result of both is the same. Man dies like an animal.

How different it is for us who know that we have come from the
creative hand of God and that we are going back to God.

**Go thy way, eat thy bread with joy, and drink thy wine
with a merry heart; for God now accepteth thy works
[Eccl. 9:7].**

The do-gooder who thinks that death is the end of it all finds his joy in the "happy hour." "Drink thy wine with a merry heart." This is about the most monotonous life in the world.

> **Let thy garments be always white; and let thy head lack no ointment [Eccl. 9:8].**

He dresses up and keeps up a good front.

> **Live joyfully with the wife whom thou lovest all the days of the life of thy vanity, which he hath given thee under the sun, all the days of thy vanity: for that is thy portion in this life, and in thy labour which thou takest under the sun [Eccl. 9:9].**

Enjoy your marriage, he advises. There are many non-Christian couples who are enjoying their lives together—I have met several of them. Oh, they have their problems and their dark days, but their attitude is, "Let's make the best of it."

Now here is another verse on which the theory of soul sleep is based.

> **Whatsoever thy hand findeth to do, do it with thy might; for there is no work, nor device, nor knowledge, nor wisdom, in the grave, whither thou goest [Eccl. 9:10].**

It is certainly true that the body in the grave can no longer hold a hammer in its hand. The brain is no longer able to study or perform any mental chores. Solomon is speaking only of the body. "Whatsoever they *hand* findeth to do, do it with thy might." He is talking about the hand, not the soul. It is the hand that will be put into the grave. If you are a child of God, you will go into the presence of the Lord. If you are not a child of God, you will go to the place of the dead until you are raised to be judged at the great White Throne. This life does not end it all. This book does not teach soul sleep.

Now he will deal with social injustice and the minority groups.

> **I returned, and saw under the sun, that the race is not to the swift, nor the battle to the strong, neither yet bread to the wise, nor yet riches to men of understanding, nor yet favour to men of skill; but time and chance happeneth to them all [Eccl. 9:11].**

The observation of the man under the sun leads him to believe that life is a matter of time and chance. It is nothing but a big lottery. If you happen to be born black, you will have your problems. If you are born white, you will have your problems. If you are born yellow, you will have your problems. It's all chance, and there is nothing you can do about it. That is the thought here.

> **For man also knoweth not his time: as the fishes that are taken in an evil net, and as the birds that are caught in the snare; so are the sons of men snared in an evil time, when it falleth suddenly upon them [Eccl. 9:12].**

If time and chance are the regulators of life, then you are just as helpless as the fish caught in a net. This is an awful viewpoint, the worst kind of fatalism. This is the philosophy of the men I mentioned who fly home at the end of the week, coming back to Southern California from Dallas, Kansas City, Chicago, and Seattle. They sit in the airplane and grit their teeth in the midst of the turbulence of a storm and say, "If the plane is going to go down, it will go down. If my number comes up, there is nothing I can do about it." A man is just like a fish caught in a net. For the do-gooder, there is no other explanation. He is forced to come to this fatalistic philosophy.

Now Solomon gives a little parable:

> **There was a little city, and few men within it; and there came a great king against it, and besieged it, and built great bulwarks against it [Eccl. 9:14].**

Come a little closer, Mr. Marxist, and listen to this parable. Do you want to lift up the burden of the downtrodden? Do you want to defend a minority group and the cause of the underdog? Is that the thing you're interested in? Well, may I say to you, there will arise a dictator. "A great king" will come against a people that let down their defenses and spend all their time with social problems which unsaved men *cannot* solve. (They've had probably six thousand years or longer, and they have not yet solved the problems of life. How much longer do you think God ought to give man to work these out?) "A great king" will take over such a city when socialistic methods are adopted.

> **Now there was found in it a poor wise man, and he by his wisdom delivered the city; yet no man remembered that same poor man [Eccl. 9:15].**

Who was that man who came and brought deliverance? His name was Wisdom, and *Wisdom* is another name for Christ. He came to this earth in poverty. Jesus could actually say, ". . . The foxes have holes, and the birds of the air have nests; but the Son of man hath not where to lay his head" (Matt. 8:20). He was a poor man.

> **Then said I, Wisdom is better than strength: nevertheless the poor man's wisdom is despised, and his words are not heard.**
> **The words of wise men are heard in quiet more than the cry of him that ruleth among fools [Eccl. 9:16–17].**

Eventually the voice of the Lord Jesus will prevail. When He comes, His voice will be like the shout of the archangel and like the sound of a trumpet. There is a babble of voices in this world today, but there is coming a time when His voice will prevail in this world.

> **Wisdom is better than weapons of war: but one sinner destroyeth much good [Eccl. 9:18].**

Here is his conclusion of all he has said in this chapter. "Wisdom is better than weapons of war." And Christ is better than atomic energy.

"Wisdom is better than weapons of war." Years ago I crossed the ocean in the H.M.S. *Queen Mary,* and I shall never forget the morning when we came into Southampton. I got up early to watch it. It was a tremendous feat to bring that great ship into port. The pilot had brought her across the trackless ocean. How had he done it? He had done it by the principles that were set down by a little-known Greek philosopher years ago working in geometry. That's the way it was done. "Wisdom is better than weapons of war."

"But one sinner destroyeth much good." There is a tremendous influence exerted by the life of one individual. And the influence is more potent when it is in the wrong direction. History will bear this out.

Adam sinned and his sin has affected the entire race of mankind. Achan sinned, and because of him an entire nation went down in defeat. They had to deal with the sin of Achan before they could achieve a victory. Rehoboam's sin split the kingdom of Israel. The sin of Ananias and Sapphira brought the first defect into the early church, and from that day on the church has not been as potent as it was in the beginning.

You and I have an influence, either for good or for bad. No matter who you are, you occupy a place of influence. "For none of us liveth to himself, and no man dieth to himself" (Rom. 14:7). Every person is a preacher. No one can keep himself from being a preacher.

I made that same statement to a man, an alcoholic, who lived with his mother in a house down the street from the church. His mother was brokenhearted over her boy, and she asked me to talk to him about Christ. One day I got him into my study. He had been drinking, but he was not what you would call drunk. I told him he was breaking his mother's heart, and I told him how low down and good for nothing his life was. He was not moved; he just sat there and took it. Then I asked him, "Do you know that you are a preacher?" At that he stood up and drew back his fist—he was going to hit me. "You can't call me a preacher!" He would allow me to call him any kind of name but not a preacher! My friend, all of us are preachers. You are preaching to those around you by the life that you live.

I personally believe that the do-gooder, the man who boasts of his moral life apart from God is the greatest detriment. He actually stands in the way; he blocks the way to God because his message is, "Live like I do. I live without God. I just do good." There is nothing quite as deadening as that.

You are a preacher, whoever you are. It may be in a very small circle, but you are affecting someone. You are a preacher in your own home. This reminds me of a father who kept a jug of whiskey hidden in the corn crib. It was his habit to go out there every morning and get himself a drink. On a snowy morning he went out to the barn as was his habit, but this time he heard someone behind him. He turned around and found that it was his little son following him, stepping in the footsteps in the snow where his father had walked. The father asked, "What are you doing, son?" The boy answered, "I'm following in your footsteps." He sent the boy back into the house, and then he went out to the corn crib and smashed that jug of whiskey. He realized that he didn't want his boy to be following in his footsteps. Someone in your home is following in your footsteps. Where are you leading him?

You may be influencing a wide circle of human society. You may have influence in your neighborhood and in your community. You have influence in your Sunday School. Somebody is looking at you and watching to see whether or not you mean business with God. Does your going to church mean anything more to you than going to a drive-in to pick up a hamburger? Does your life suggest that there is a heaven to gain and a hell to shun? You have influence.

You remember that Peter preached a mighty sermon on the Day of Pentecost. Andrew just sat on the sidelines and could say, "That is my brother. I brought him to Christ." That was Andrew's influence. You, today, are pointing men to heaven or to hell. Now, if you want to go to hell, that's your business, but you have no right to lead a little boy there. You have no right to lead your family and those who surround you there. Even if you want to go, it's awful to lead others. Influence— "One sinner destroyeth much good." Think about it.

# CHAPTER 10

We see here that the injustice of life suggests the adoption of a moderate course.

**Dead flies cause the ointment of the apothecary to send forth a stinking savour: so doth a little folly him that is in reputation for wisdom and honour [Eccl. 10:1].**

Life is full of illustrations of this truth. One night on the town can mean a lifetime in the darkness of disease or even death. An officer in a church I served years ago told me, "I was brought up in a Christian home, and I really never did run around, but when I went away from home and got a job, I went out with the fellows one night. That is the only night in my life that I went out, and that is the night I got a venereal disease. I had to postpone marriage for several years, and I had to break off an engagement with a sweet, lovely girl." Just one dead fly will ruin the ointment of the apothecary. How tragic!

A mother spends twenty-one years teaching a son to be wise, and some girl will come along and make a fool out of him in five minutes. What a picture! A little folly, a little foolishness—that is all it takes. It can be the thing that can ruin a life and spoil the lives of others.

**A wise man's heart is at his right hand; but a fool's heart at his left [Eccl. 10:2].**

The right hand is the hand of strength. A wise man's heart is at his right hand. Whatever he does, he does it with all his heart. He doesn't do it reluctantly. The fool's heart is at his left hand. He just does things in a half-hearted way.

My friend, whatever you do, do it with heart. If you are going to serve God, do it with joy and excitement. Don't make the Christian life a drudge. Make it something worthwhile. Whatever you do, do it with excitement.

> **Yea also, when he that is a fool walketh by the way, his wisdom faileth him, and he saith to every one that he is a fool [Eccl. 10:3].**

A fool does not have to carry a placard on himself that says, "I am a fool." The fact of the matter is that all he has to do is open his mouth. Sometimes he doesn't even have to open his mouth to prove that he is a fool.

Sometimes at community meetings people will get up to express a viewpoint. A man will make a thoughtful suggestions, and I will think, *My, I didn't know my neighbor was so intelligent.* Then a fellow gets up to speak, and the minute he opens his mouth, I look at my friend sitting next to me and arch my eyebrows. The Bible calls him a fool, and he tells everyone what he is.

> **If the spirit of the ruler rise up against thee, leave not thy place; for yielding pacifieth great offences [Eccl. 10:4].**

The man under the sun is going to take the position of yielding in order to pacify. In other words, "If you can't fight city hall, join them."

> **There is an evil which I have seen under the sun, as an error which proceedeth from the ruler:**
>
> **Folly is set in great dignity, and the rich sit in low place [Eccl. 10:5–6].**

This is one of the things that has happened in our day and age: a dignity has been given to sin. There was a time when sin was down on the side street. It was considered dirty and filthy, and it savored of that which was low and foul. But today sin has moved up on the boulevard.

Sin is committed with great dignity, and it has been given a prominent place. It is given a prominent place on TV shows.

I noticed the other day that they interviewed a stripper on a TV show, that is, a girl who takes off her clothes in a nightclub. When I was a young fellow in my teens, living a life away from God, we would sneak off on Saturday night to go to such shows. It was dirty; it was filthy. Today they call it an art form! Today sin is handled in such a dignified way. "Folly is set in great *dignity*, and the rich sit in low place."

Have you heard interviews with the ordinary citizen or with the ordinary Christian? These are the people who are making the finest contribution to their community and to their society. Are they the ones who are interviewed? No, they occupy a low place. You never hear of them. The attention is focused on the ones who are the sinners and oddballs.

**I have seen servants upon horses, and princes walking as servants upon the earth [Eccl. 10:7].**

To work hard, save your money, and study late do not always mean that you will become a success. The fool next door may inherit a million dollars. Sometimes it is the fool who rides the horse, while the prince walks as the servant.

I know many wonderful Christians—across this land I have had the privilege of meeting some of the most wonderful people who are humble folk. Many of them live in humble homes; some of them are financially well-to-do. But they are ignored. They are "princes walking as servants upon the earth" today. What a picture!

**He that diggeth a pit shall fall into it; and whoso breaketh an hedge, a serpent shall bite him [Eccl. 10:8].**

If you think that you can get by with sin, especially if you are a child of God, you are very foolish. God may not act immediately, but all you need to do is wait; God will eventually judge you for it. I have watched that over the years. Christians do things that are wrong and seem to get by with it, but somewhere down the line God begins to move in on them, and He takes them to His woodshed.

> **Whoso removeth stones shall be hurt therewith; and he that cleaveth wood shall be endangered thereby [Eccl. 10:9].**

Removing stones in that day was removing the markers of property lines. This is saying again that one cannot get by with sin. Whatsoever a man sows, that shall he also reap. If you try to cheat someone out of his property, or anything else, God will see to it that you will get hurt. This is the reason the Lord tells us that we are not to avenge ourselves. The Lord says, ". . . Vengeance is mine; I will repay . . ." (Rom. 12:19). The Lord is the One who will settle the accounts.

> **If the iron be blunt, and he do not whet the edge, then must he put to more strength: but wisdom is profitable to direct [Eccl. 10:10].**

If the hoe gets dull, you will sharpen it, if you have any sense at all. A dull hoe makes digging that much harder. Unfortunately, many people are not willing to do the thing that will sharpen the hoe.

A young man told me the other day that God had called him to preach, and he wanted to take a short course to prepare himself. I said, "Young man, don't do that. Sharpen your hoe. Sharpen your sword. Don't go out untrained. Take the time for sharpening." It is foolish to take out a dull hoe and expect to cut down many weeds. Sharpen the hoe and then move in on the weed patch. The Book of Ecclesiastes has some great lessons for us to learn. It is an unusual book.

> **Surely the serpent will bite without enchantment; and a babbler is not better [Eccl. 10:11].**

We need to understand the practices of the East if we are going to understand this verse. It is very similar to Psalm 58:4–5: "Their poison is like the poison of a serpent: they are like the deaf adder that stoppeth her ear; Which will not hearken to the voice of charmers, charming never so wisely." The same idea is found in Jeremiah. "For, behold, I will send serpents, cockatrices, among you, which will not be charmed, and they shall bite you, saith the LORD" (Jer. 8:17).

The adder is a very deadly reptile. We have all seen pictures of the Indian fakirs (and I believe it would be just as correct to spell it *fakers*) who play a doleful sort of tune on a horn to charm the cobra. The cobra does a sort of dance; I suppose one could call it the cobra hula dance. The cobra will not strike as long as the tune is being played on that horn. Now I don't know about you, but if I had one of those horns, and a cobra came along, I'd be a long-winded person—I'd play as long as I possibly could. But there will come a time when the cobra or the adder will not listen, and finally he will strike. When he does strike, it means death.

The "serpent" in the passages we have quoted probably is not referring to literal snakes. I think it is referring to that person, "babbler," who will deceive you, who will betray you, a Judas Iscariot. After all, that's what Antichrist will be to the nation of Israel in the great Tribulation Period.

Even among people in the church you will find those who will say things that are not true. "Surely the serpent will bite without enchantment; and a babbler is not better." He may pose as your friend, but he is going to bite you like a serpent no matter how nice you are to him.

This was the kind of sorrow that David felt when his friend Ahithophel turned against him. Ahithophel had been his counselor and his personal friend, but he left David and went with Absalom when Absalom rebelled. That broke David's heart. I think David was a broken man after the rebellion of Absalom. Up to that time, I doubt that there had ever been a ruler like king David in his prime. After that time of rebellion David became an old man. He pours out his heart in Psalm 55, and this is the picture we get.

Solomon is saying that in view of the possibility of this happening, one should be very careful. I would say that that is the philosophy of life of the average person today. He is the do-gooder who walks in the middle of the road. He has been told to be careful with So-and-So, who can repeat what he says and twist it. So when Mr. Do-gooder faces these people he adopts a very sweet attitude toward them, but he is very careful about what he says.

Sometimes it seems that we actually should confront the kind of person who takes facts and twists them and point out to that person exactly what he or she is doing. However, I know from experience that if you point this out, you will be attacked in a most vicious manner.

> **The words of a wise man's mouth are gracious; but the lips of a fool will swallow up himself [Eccl. 10:12].**

"The lips of a fool will swallow up himself" and those who are around him as well. That is why one should be careful in making friends and choosing the right kind of friends. When I taught school, I always advised the freshman class, "You are going to make friends here that will be friends with you for life. You may even meet your mate here (and of course some of them did), so be careful about the friends you make."

When my daughter went away to college, I gave her that same advice. I told her she would have the greatest opportunity of all her life to make some wonderful friendships. But I advised her to be careful in choosing her friends. There are some people who will try to destroy you.

There are people who are like the adder or the serpent. If you are nice to them and can keep them charmed, things will go well, but be very careful how you act in their presence. This is good advice, my friend, but it is a middle-of-the-road course, as you can see.

> **The beginning of the words of his mouth is foolishness: and the end of his talk is mischievous madness.**
>
> **A fool also is full of words: a man cannot tell what shall be; and what shall be after him, who can tell him? [Eccl. 10:13–14].**

How true this is. Have you ever noticed that if you have a group and you throw out a topic for an open discussion, there will generally be some loquacious person in that group. (I believe that now they call such sessions "rap" sessions. When I was young, we called them "bull" sessions.) Usually some person who likes to talk will take over the discussion, and often he will say foolish, absurd things. The group begins to wish that person would keep his mouth shut.

This is one reason why I am not very fond of open discussions. When I have a question and answer period, I always encourage people to write out their questions. If you don't do that, you will almost invariably find one babbler in the group, one talker who comes under this category of being a troublemaker. Someone has described such a person as one whose brain starts his mouth working, and then the brain goes off and leaves it.

**The labour of the foolish wearieth every one of them, because he knoweth not how to go to the city [Eccl. 10:15].**

Today we would say the fool doesn't know enough to come in out of the rain.

**Woe to thee, O land, when thy king is a child, and thy princes eat in the morning! [Eccl. 10:16].**

They give themselves over to pleasure instead of ruling the people properly and being a blessing to the land.

**Blessed art thou, O land, when thy king is the son of nobles, and thy princes eat in due season, for strength, and not for drunkenness! [Eccl. 10:17].**

The big problem in our country is not drugs but liquor. The number of alcoholics in this country is now in the millions. Probably we cannot get an accurate figure on the number of alcoholics because of the liquor interests, but it is a real cause for alarm. There are too many cocktail parties in Washington where the political decisions are being made. "Blessed art thou, O land, when . . . thy princes eat in due season, for strength, and not for drunkenness!"

**By much slothfulness the building decayeth; and through idleness of the hands the house droppeth through [Eccl. 10:18].**

This is an indictment of laziness, of the refusal to work. I'm afraid that is becoming a way of life in our country today. A common greeting is, "Take it easy" and "Have a good day." In other words, do as little as possible and have as much fun as you can.

**A feast is made for laughter, and wine maketh merry: but money answereth all things [Eccl. 10:19].**

Many of the rich have moved to the middle of the road. They want to be liberal and yet they want to be conservative.

**Curse not the king, no not in thy thought; and curse not the rich in thy bedchamber: for a bird of the air shall carry the voice, and that which hath wings shall tell the matter [Eccl. 10:20].**

"Curse not the king." Regardless of our president's political party or his views, I do not feel that he should be caricatured or made an object of ridicule. In the New Testament Peter says, ". . . Honour the king" (1 Pet. 2:17).

# CHAPTER 11

This chapter gives the best course to follow for the do-gooder, for the moral man, the man who wants to live the good life and wants to go down the middle, neither hot nor cold, neither right nor left.

> **Cast thy bread upon the waters: for thou shalt find it after many days [Eccl. 11:1].**

Don't be afraid of doing good although the reward may be late in arriving.

> **Give a portion to seven, and also to eight; for thou knowest not what evil shall be upon the earth [Eccl. 11:2].**

When you are doing good, be sure to help more than one person. Help quite a few people because you may get into trouble yourself at some later time, and there will be many people who will be willing to help you.

The Lord Jesus told a parable along this line, and it is recorded in Luke 16. There was an "unjust" steward who was really a crook. He made friends for himself by reducing their debts to his master, so that when he lost his job he could go to them for help.

> **If the clouds be full of rain, they empty themselves upon the earth: and if the tree fall toward the south, or toward the north, in the place where the tree falleth, there it shall be [Eccl. 11:3].**

If rain is predicted, you had better carry an umbrella. After a big redwood tree falls, it is hard to move it. What is he saying here? It is best to have a clear understanding of a situation at the very beginning before you launch a venture because, after it begins, it is very difficult to make any change.

**He that observeth the wind shall not sow; and he that regardeth the clouds shall not reap [Eccl. 11:4].**

That is, act wisely in what you do. If a man wants to sow seed, he had better wait until there is no wind. If a man wants to reap a harvest, he will not begin if rain is threatening.

**As thou knowest not what is the way of the spirit, nor how the bones do grow in the womb of her that is with child: even so thou knowest not the works of God who maketh all [Eccl. 11:5].**

The formation of the fetus and the physical birth of a baby are still great mysteries today. Spiritual rebirth is an even greater mystery. You do not know how the Spirit will move. The Lord Jesus said that. "The wind bloweth where it listeth, and thou hearest the sound thereof, but canst not tell whence it cometh, and whither it goeth: so is every one that is born of the Spirit" (John 3:8). There is a great deal that we do not know.

I believe his point is simply this: Don't let what you don't know disturb what you do know. Let me give an example. Any person knows enough to sit in a chair. There is an empty chair in my study right now. I don't mind getting up and going over there to sit down. Now there are a lot of things I don't know about that chair. I don't know anything about its construction—who made it or how it was made—but I do know that I can sit in that chair and it will hold me up. That is really all I need to know about the chair. So don't let what you don't know disturb what you do know.

**Truly the light is sweet, and a pleasant thing it is for the eyes to behold the sun:**

> But if a man live many years, and rejoice in them all; yet let him remember the days of darkness; for they shall be many. All that cometh is vanity [Eccl. 11:7-8].

Some day you will get old, my friend. Life for the senior citizen is not always as pleasant as the advertising folders say it is going to be.

> Rejoice, O young man, in thy youth; and let thy heart cheer thee in the days of thy youth, and walk in the ways of thine heart, and in the sight of thine eyes: but know thou, that for all these things God will bring thee into judgment.

> Therefore remove sorrow from thy heart, and put away evil from thy flesh: for childhood and youth are vanity [Eccl. 11:9-10].

Remember, young man, now is the time to make your decisions in every category of life. It is very important that you make the right choices now. How many men have lived wasted lives and are living them today because they made the wrong choices in their youth.

Your youthful days are empty if they are not lived right. Life is a gift that is given to us by God, given one day at a time, in fact, one second at a time. It is a precious gift, and it is to be used for the glory of God. What is the chief end of man? The chief end of man is to glorify God and to enjoy Him forever.

# CHAPTER 12

We have seen the experiments that Solomon made in life. He is probably the only man who ever lived who was able to experiment in all of these different areas, attempting to find a solution and satisfaction apart from God. Throughout Ecclesiastes the key expression has been "under the sun." He tried nature and natural science as his first experiment.

A great many people today feel that they will solve their problems by getting back to nature. There is a great exodus out of the cities and into the suburbs and beyond the suburbs to a little cabin by a lake or by a river or up in the mountains. "Let's get away from it all. Let's get back to nature." Well, this didn't solve Solomon's problems, and it will not solve our problems. So Solomon tried wisdom and philosophy; he tried pleasure and materialism; he experimented with fatalism; he tried living life for self. He turned to religion and found ritual but no reality. Then he tried to find the answer in wealth. Finally Solomon tried the good life, the life of the moralist, which he found to be an insipid sort of existence. I think that is why the young people today rebel against it.

Solomon now comes to his final conclusion in this chapter.

## POETIC PICTURE OF OLD AGE

This chapter is going to have something for the young person and for the senior citizen. Both ends of the spectrum of life meet here.

> **Remember now thy Creator in the days of thy youth, while the evil days come not, nor the years draw nigh, when thou shalt say, I have no pleasure in them [Eccl. 12:1].**

In view of the fact that nothing under the sun can satisfy the human heart, Solomon says, "Get back to God." While you are young, make your decision for God. It is going to be obvious why this should be done.

Solomon will paint a picture of old age, and it is not a pretty picture. Nevertheless, it is your picture and my picture in old age. When I first preached on this chapter of Ecclesiastes, I was a very young preacher, and I wondered if it would really be like this. Now I am here to testify that the description of old age in Ecclesiastes is accurate.

One often hears the liberal and the skeptic say, "I believe in a religion of the here and now. I'm not interested in a religion of the hereafter." Well, here is a religion for the "here," which means to get rightly related to God and live for Him. Why? Well, let's look at this picture he paints of old age—a tremendous picture.

**While the sun, or the light, or the moon, or the stars, be not darkened, nor the clouds return after the rain [Eccl. 12:2].**

Does he mean that the sun, the moon, the stars, the lights are all going out? No, he means that you don't see them as you used to.

Mrs. McGee and I took a walk when we were in the Hawaiian Islands, under a full moon, and it was beautiful. I said to her, "My, isn't that a beautiful moon? But you know, it doesn't seem as romantic as it once did. How do you feel?" She replied, "No, I don't think it is as romantic as it once was. I used to think Hawaii was the most romantic place in the world." Well, my friend, when you get old, the luster dims.

Time flies, and one sad experience follows another—"the clouds return after the rain." When you get old, you can go out and have a great day but, believe me, you must take three or four days to rest up afterward. I have learned that.

I used to have a heavy schedule of conferences and just kept on going and enjoying every minute of it. Now Mrs. McGee and I find that we need to change our whole life-style. Conferences are becoming wearing on us. "The clouds return after the rain."

**In the day when the keepers of the house shall tremble, and the strong men shall bow themselves, and the grinders cease because they are few, and those that look out of the windows be darkened [Eccl. 12:3].**

This is the description of the body, the physical body, in old age. "The keepers of the house shall tremble." These are the legs. The old person begins to totter.

My staff and my close friends try to kid me by saying, "Oh, you're looking so strong and so well." Yet I notice when I get in and out of a car, they are at my elbow to help me. Do you know why? Because my legs don't move quite as fast as they once did.

When I get up in the morning and come down the steps, I groan. My wife gets after me and asks, "Why do you groan?" I tell her it is scriptural to groan. Paul tells us, "For we that are in this tabernacle do groan, being burdened . . ." (2 Cor. 5:4). So I tell her that I want to be scriptural. But honestly I groan because my knees hurt when I come down the steps. "The keepers of the house shall tremble."

I find that I stumble more than I used to, and I must be more careful when I climb a ladder. An old person gets himself a walking stick, and I've been thinking about that, too.

"And the strong men shall bow themselves." Those are the shoulders. They are no longer erect. My wife told me the other day, "You'd look lots better if you would stand erect like you used to stand. When you were young, you had broad shoulders, and now you are all stooped over." Well, friend, the "strong men" are bowing themselves. They don't stay back like they once did. The shoulders begin to round off, and I can assure you it is more comfortable that way.

"The grinders cease because they are few." The grinders are the teeth. You are going to lose your teeth as you get older. You will need to have some bridges put in or full dentures. I haven't had to resort to false teeth yet—I'm thankful I still have my own—but they have all been capped now for years.

"Those that look out of the windows be darkened" refers to failing eyesight. The other night in a restaurant a man came up to me, we shook hands, and I talked with that man for two minutes before I even recognized who he was. I just couldn't place him. I met another friend at a meeting. We talked a while and after he left, I asked my wife who he was. She told me his name. It was a man whom I had known for years. I said, "To tell you the truth, I didn't know him. He surely has changed." She said, "Yes, I think he has, but you have too." So you see that the windows get darkened. Even with my trifocals, I don't see as well as I did. Things don't look quite as bright as they once did.

**And the doors shall be shut in the streets, when the sound of the grinding is low, and he shall rise up at the voice of the bird, and all the daughters of music shall be brought low [Eccl. 12:4].**

"The doors shall be shut in the streets" means that the hearing is failing. My wife tells friends, "You'll have to speak a little louder. He's getting hard of hearing." I'm not really, by the way. She says that I often don't hear what she says. Maybe sometimes it is that I don't want to hear. Several years ago I had a neighbor who wore a hearing device. His wife would get after him when he got out to trim trees or prune his fruit trees. He would be up on the ladder working, and she would come out and rebuke him for it. All he did was take out his hearing aid. She would talk to him for fifteen minutes, and he wouldn't hear a word she said. Finally she would say, "I don't think you are wearing your hearing aid," and he wasn't. He would just keep on doing what he wanted to do.

Well, noise, even out on the street, is not as loud as it once was. "The doors shall be shut in the streets." And "when the sound of grinding is low." The grinding is literally the grinding women. They don't seem to make as much noise as they used to.

"He shall rise up at the voice of the bird." I can remember when I was a boy that even a loud alarm clock wouldn't wake me up in the morning. When my wife and I were young, we didn't mind the noise of children. We didn't mind the noise of music coming from the neighbors. We could sleep in motels and hotels, and none of the noises bothered us. Now even the little chirp of a bird disturbs us! Now when we travel and we come to a motel or hotel I always ask, "Can you give us a quiet room?" We are getting old, and we rise up at the voice of the bird. Any little noise disturbs our sleep.

"And all the daughters of music shall be brought low." You don't find too many older people singing in the choir anymore. The voice gets thin, and it gets harder to carry a tune. I remember dear brother Homer Rodeheaver. What a marvelous music director and song leader he was! I remember him as a young man when he traveled with Billy Sunday. How he thrilled me when I heard him as a boy. He played the trombone, sang, and led the singing. What a voice he had! Then I invited him to come to the church I pastored in downtown Los Angeles. He was in his seventies by then. I would help him up, and he would go tottering up to the platform. He was still a marvelous song leader; I don't think anyone could ever excel him. But every now and then he would sing a stanza, and my feeling was that he would have done better to *read* the stanza. It was no longer the glorious voice that we had heard years before.

Even the people who once had beautiful singing voices lose the quality of their voices as they get older. Those of us who never could see very well should realize that we had better praise the Lord in our *hearts*. That is the reason I never open my mouth in a song service. I don't dare. I couldn't sing when I was young, and now it is positively frightful. "The daughters of music shall be brought low."

Now he continues on as he speaks of old age. And now, to me, it gets to the place where it's tragic because we're looking at the psychological effects.

**Also when they shall be afraid of that which is high, and fears shall be in the way, and the almond tree shall flourish, and the grasshopper shall be a burden, and desire shall fail: because man goeth to his long home, and the mourners go about the streets [Eccl. 12:5].**

"They shall be afraid of that which is high." I never did enjoy flying, but I was getting over my fear and beginning to enjoy it. Then old age slipped up on me, and I find today I have the same old fear of flying that I had at the very beginning. Little things disturb me, little things that didn't disturb me at all when I was younger.

"And fears shall be in the way." We just don't enjoy things as much as we once did. We have always enjoyed traveling and have conducted many tours to the Bible lands and to the Hawaiian Islands. I have noticed that as we and our friends get older, we find traveling much more difficult. We worry and wonder about things we never even thought of before.

When we were young, my wife and I would start out in an old jalopy to go across the country. We never made any reservations. It didn't worry us if we stopped at motels and found that they were all filled. It didn't bother us if we had to sleep on the side of the road. But today there is always a nagging fear. When we get ready to make a trip, I have all the reservations made well in advance, and I go over the road map again and again and again. "Fears shall be in the way."

"The almond tree shall flourish." A blossoming almond tree is white. And the senior citizen is going to turn white on top, or else there won't be anything left on the top—it is one or the other.

"The grasshopper shall be a burden." How can a little grasshopper be a burden? Well, when old age comes, little things that never used to bother now become a burden. We love our grandchildren dearly and enjoy having them with us, but after a while, we are glad to see them go home again. Strength fails, endurance fails, patience fails. Many *little* things become a burden.

"Desire shall fail." Romance is gone. You can try to act as if you are just as young as you were, but you don't fool anyone. I remember listening to an evangelist who had married a young girl. He hopped on the platform, jumped in the air, and said, "I'm just as young as I ever was." He wasn't fooling anybody but himself, and he died shortly after that.

"Because man goeth to his long home, and the mourners go about the streets." That "long home" is eternity. Death is getting near.

**Or ever the silver cord be loosed, or the golden bowl be broken, or the pitcher be broken at the fountain, or the wheel broken at the cistern [Eccl. 12:6].**

Here is a list of the organs of the body. At the end, they no longer function. The "silver cord" is the spinal cord. The "golden bowl" is the head, the bowl for the brain. The functioning of the brain decreases in its efficiency as one gets older, and at death it ceases to function at all. The pitcher is the lungs. "The pitcher is broken at the fountain." The wheel is the heart—"the wheel broken at the cistern." It is no longer pumping blood through the body. All of this is a picture of the deterioration of old age leading to death. Life cannot be sustained without the functioning of these organs.

**Then shall the dust return to the earth as it was: and the spirit shall return unto God who gave it [Eccl. 12:7].**

There is no soul sleep. I wish the people who try to use verses from this Book of Ecclesiastes to support their idea of soul sleep would just read on until they get to this verse. The body sleeps, but the spirit, or the soul, returns unto God who gave it.

Let me repeat that the New Testament assures us that to be absent from the body means to be present with the Lord (see 2 Cor. 5:8). The soul immediately returns to God. This body is just a tabernacle, or a tent, that we live in. It is just the outer covering. The soul goes to be with God.

When President Adams became an old man, someone asked him how he was getting along. His reply was something like this: "Oh, I'm doing fine, but this house I live in is growing very feeble, and I think I'll be moving out of it before long." That was true. He did move out of his old house shortly after that.

**Vanity of vanities, saith the preacher; all is vanity [Eccl. 12:8].**

Young man, life is empty if you are just living for the here and now. One day you will find that all you have in your hand is a fistful of ashes, and you will have eternity ahead of you.

When as a child, I laughed and wept,
  Time crept;
When as a youth, I dreamed and talked,
  Time walked;
When I became a full grown man,
  Time ran;
When older still I daily grew,
  Time flew;
Soon I shall find in traveling on,
  Time gone.
                          —Author unknown

The psalmist writes, "So teach us to number our days, that we may apply our hearts unto wisdom" (Ps. 90:12), and Wisdom is the Lord Jesus Christ.

Thinking of old age, someone has written this bit of whimsey:

Thou knowest, Lord, I'm growing older.
My fire of youth begins to smolder;

I somehow tend to reminisce
And speak of good old days I miss.

I am more moody, bossy, and
Think folk should jump at my
    command.

Help me, Lord, to conceal my aches
And realize my own mistakes.

Keep me sweet, silent, sane, serene,
Instead of crusty, sour, and mean.
                          —Author unknown

May the Lord give us the grace to grow old gracefully.

> And moreover, because the preacher was wise, he still taught the people knowledge; yea, he gave good heed, and sought out, and set in order many proverbs.
>
> The preacher sought to find out acceptable words: and that which was written was upright, even words of truth.
>
> The words of the wise are as goads, and as nails fastened by the masters of assemblies, which are given from one shepherd [Eccl. 12:9–11].

We should not by any means despise the wisdom of the past, nor should we refuse to be taught.

> And further, by these, my son, be admonished: of making many books there is no end; and much study is a weariness of the flesh [Eccl. 12:12].

Education will not solve the problems of life.

## THE RESULT OF THE EXPERIMENT

> Let us hear the conclusion of the whole matter: Fear God, and keep his commandments: for this is the whole duty of man [Eccl. 12:13].

"Fear God." This is the message of the Book of Proverbs as well as the message here. In view of the experiment made "under the sun," the wise thing is to fear God, which means to reverence, worship, and obey Him.

"And keep his commandments" would mean to meet God's conditions for salvation—in any age—grounded on faith in God. For Cain it meant bringing a lamb. For Abraham it meant believing the promises of God. For the people of Israel it meant approaching God through sacrifice in the tabernacle and in the temple. For us it is to ". . . Believe on the Lord Jesus Christ, and thou shalt be saved . . ." (Acts 16:31).

**For God shall bring every work into judgment, with
every secret thing, whether it be good, or whether it be
evil [Eccl. 12:14].**

"For God shall bring every work into judgment." God will judge every
man, for every man is a sinner who is guilty before God. Christ bore
our judgment; He died a judgment death. Our sins are either on Christ
by faith in Him, or else we must come before the Great White Throne
for judgment.

"Remember now thy Creator in the days of thy youth." Why? Well,
for a very definite reason: because in the matter of salvation your
chances of being saved are greater; and in the subject of service you'll
have something to offer to God. Statistics show that more come to
Christ when they are young.

This does not mean that old people cannot accept Christ and be
saved. On one of our radio programs we gave an invitation for those
who wanted to accept Christ to put up their hands. A lady walked into
the room where her ninety-year-old father was listening to the program, and she saw that he sat there in the rocking chair listening to us
with his hand in the air. When she questioned him, she found that he
had accepted Christ Jesus as his Savior. How wonderful! It is never too
late.

The second reason why Solomon makes a special appeal to young
people is that they have a lifetime to offer to God in service to Him. The
men who have had real service, who have had something to give to
God, have been young men: Joseph, Moses, Gideon, David, Jeremiah,
Saul of Tarsus, Timothy—and oh, the host of young missionaries in
the past few centuries such as Robert Moffat, who was "wee Bobby
Moffat" when he came to Christ as a child and became a great missionary to South Africa.

My friend, there is no answer to the problems of life "under the
sun." Jesus Christ is the only solution of the problems of life. The Lord
Jesus has given His promise to people of any and all ages: ". . . him that
cometh to me I will in no wise cast out" (John 6:37).

# BIBLIOGRAPHY

## (Recommended for Further Study)

Darby, J. N. *Synopsis of the Books of the Bible.* Addison, Illinois: Bible Truth Publishers.

DeHaan, Richard W. *The Art of Staying Off Dead-End Streets.* Grand Rapids, Michigan: Radio Bible Class, 1974. (A study in Ecclesiastes)

Gaebelein, Arno C. *The Annotated Bible.* 1917. Reprint. Neptune, New Jersey: Loizeaux Brothers, 1971.

Goldberg, Louis. *Ecclesiastes.* Grand Rapids, Michigan: Zondervan Publishing House, 1983.

Gray, James M. *Commentary on the Whole Bible.* Old Tappan, New Jersey: Fleming H. Revell Co., 1906.

Jennings, F. C. *Meditations on Ecclesiastes.* Sunbury, Pennsylvania: Believer's Bookshelf, 1920.

Jensen, Irving L. *Ecclesiastes and the Song of Solomon.* Chicago, Illinois: Moody Press, 1974. (A self-study guide)

Kaiser, Walter C. Jr. *Ecclesiastes: Total Life.* Chicago, Illinois: Moody Press, 1979.

Unger, Merrill F. *Unger's Bible Handbook.* Chicago, Illinois: Moody Press, 1966.

Unger, Merrill F. *Unger's Commentary on the Old Testament.* Vol. I. Chicago, Illinois: Moody Press, 1981.

# SONG OF SOLOMON

# The
# SONG OF SOLOMON

## INTRODUCTION

The first verse of this little book identifies Solomon as its writer: "The song of songs, which is Solomon's." Solomon also wrote the Books of Proverbs and Ecclesiastes.

This book is actually not a story at all; it is a song. We read in 1 Kings 4:32: "And he [Solomon] spake three thousand proverbs: and his songs were a thousand and five." Solomon wrote three thousand proverbs, but it is quite interesting that if you count the proverbs in the Book of Proverbs and even include the Book of Ecclesiastes, you come up with quite a few less than three thousand. So we have very few of all that Solomon wrote. However, we can say two things about those that we do have: first, we have the best that he wrote—surely we would have that; second, we have those that the Spirit of God wanted us to have.

This verse also tells us that "his songs were a thousand and five." Think of that—more than a thousand songs! That makes him quite a songwriter. He would have fit in on Tin Pan Alley any day. It is interesting to note that the Word of God is very specific when it says that he wrote one thousand *and five* songs. It doesn't simply give us a round number. Probably those which have been preserved for us are those five. Most of Solomon's songs, of course, we do not have. In fact, we generally say that we have only one song. But the Song of Solomon is also called the Book of Canticles. A canticle is a little song, and that means that in this book we have several canticles, several little songs. There is a difference of opinion as to how many songs there are. The old position is that there are five, and I agree with that. I notice that *The New Scofield Reference Bible* states that there are thirteen. That is an excellent Bible, but I will continue to accept the old division of the book into five songs.

"Beloved" is the name for Him; "love" is the name for her.

"I am my beloved's, and my beloved is mine: he feedeth among the lilies" (Song 6:3).

"Many waters cannot quench love, neither can the floods drown it: if a man would give all the substance of his house for love, it would utterly be contemned" (Song 8:7).

The Song of Solomon is a parabolic poem. The *interpretation*, not the inspiration, causes the difficulty. There are some who actually feel it should not be in the Bible; however, it is in the canon of Scripture. The Song of Solomon is the great neglected book of the Bible. The reader who is going through the Word of God for the first time is puzzled when he comes to it. The carnal Christian will misunderstand and misinterpret it. Actually this little book has been greatly abused by people who have not understood it. When Peter was puzzled by some of Paul's epistles, he wrote, "As also in all his epistles, speaking in them of these things; in which are some things hard to be understood, which they that are unlearned and unstable wrest, as they do also the other scriptures, unto their own destruction" (2 Pet. 3:16). I think this is also true of the Song of Solomon.

Origen and Jerome tell us that the Jews would not permit their young men to read this book until they were thirty years old. The reason was that they felt there was the danger of reading into it the salacious and the suggestive, the vulgar and the voluptuous, the sensuous and the sexual. On the contrary, this is a wonderful picture of physical, human, wedded love. It gives the answer to two erroneous groups of people: those who hold to asceticism and think it is wrong to get married, and those who hold to hedonism and think that the satisfying of their lusts is of primary importance. This book makes it very clear that both are wrong. It upholds wedded love as a very wonderful thing, a glorious experience.

Sometimes young preachers are counseled not to use the Song of Solomon until they become old men. A retired minister advised me not to preach on it until I was sixty years old. Do you know what I did? I turned right around and preached on it immediately—that's what a young preacher would do. Now that I am past sixty years, I think I am qualified, at least as far as the chronology is concerned, to be able to speak on it. This book means more to me today than it did forty years ago. The elaborate, vivid, striking, and bold language in this book is a wonderful, glorious picture of our relationship with the Lord Jesus Christ. I know of no book that will draw you closer to Him or be more personal than the Song of Solomon.

If you were to compare the Song of Solomon with other Oriental poetry of its period—such as some of the Persian poetry—you would find the Song of Solomon to be mild and restrained. Reading the Persian poetry, on the other hand, would be like reading some of the modern, dirty stuff that is being written today.

By contrast, the Jews called the Song of Solomon the Holy of Holies of Scripture. Therefore, not everyone was permitted inside its sacred enclosure. Here is where you are dwelling in the secret place of the Most High. That is one reason I hesitate to discuss this book. It will be abused by unbelievers and carnal Christians. But if you are one who is walking with the Lord, if the Lord Jesus mans a great deal to you and you love Him, then this little book will mean a great deal to you also.

The Song of Solomon is poetic and practical. Here God is speaking to His people in poetic songs which unfold a story. We need to take our spiritual shoes from off our feet as we approach this book. We are on holy ground. The Song of Solomon is like a fragile flower that requires delicate handling.

There have been four different and important meanings found in this book:

1. The Song of Solomon sets forth *the glory of wedded love*. Here is declared the sacredness of the marital relationship and that marriage is a God-given institution. This little book shows us what real love is.

The Jews taught that it reveals the heart of a satisfied husband and that of a devoted wife.

Today we see a great movement toward "sexual freedom," which many people seem to think is good. One young man who had lived and believed in "free love" told me that he had come to realize that such a life is the life of an animal. He said, "For several years I lived like an animal. If you want to know the truth, I don't think sex means any more to my group of friends than it means to an animal." The younger generation today is geared to sex; their life style is one of sexual expression. But I am of the opinion that they actually know very little about it. All they know about sex is what an animal knows. A dog out on the street knows as much as they do. Something is missing— there is a terrible void in their lives.

This generation may have a great deal of experience with sex but knows little about love. They know the Hollywood version of love; yet they think they know it all. The story is told of the father who wanted to talk to his young boy about sex. He beat around the bush and finally blurted out, "Son, I'd like to talk to you about some of the facts of life." The boy said, "Sure, Dad, what would you like to know?" The boy knew the raw facts about sex, so he thought he knew more than his dad knew. There was a veteran movie queen who had had five husbands. She knew about sex, but she didn't know anything about real love; so she committed suicide. Reading our modern novels and plays is like taking a trip through the sewers of Paris! There is a stark contrast between the ideas of our generation and the glory of wedded love as it is portrayed in the Song of Solomon.

2. This little book sets forth *the love of Jehovah for Israel*. That is not a new thought which is found in this book alone. The prophets spoke of Israel as the wife of Jehovah. Hosea dwells on that theme. Idolatry in Israel is likened to a breach in wedded love and is the greatest sin in all the world according to Hosea.

The scribes and the rabbis of Israel have always given these two interpretations to this book, and they have been accepted by the church. However, there are two other interpretations set forth by the church.

3. The Song of Solomon is *a picture of Christ and the church*. The church is the bride of Christ. This is a familiar figure in the New Testament (see Eph. 5; Rev. 21). However, in this book God uses a picture of human affection to convey to our dull minds, our dead hearts, our distorted affections, and our diseased wills His so great love. He uses the very best of human love to arouse us to realize the wonderful love that He has for us. This book can lead you into a marvelous, wonderful relationship with the Lord Jesus which you probably have never known before. My friend, what we need today is a knowledge of the Word of God and a personal relationship with Jesus Christ. I am afraid that very few of us are experiencing this today.

4. This book depicts *the communion of Christ and the individual believer*. It portrays the love of Christ for the individual and the soul's communion with Christ. Many great saints of God down through the years have experienced this. Paul could say, ". . . the Son of God, who loved me, and gave himself for me" (Gal. 2:20). Samuel Rutherford could spend a whole night in prayer. His wife would miss him during the night and would get up and go looking for him. Even on cold nights she would find him on his knees praying, and she would take his big overcoat and throw it around him. Men like Dwight L. Moody and Robert McCheyne came into a real, personal relationship with the Lord Jesus Christ. This is not some kind of second experience, as some people try to describe it. It is more than an experience. It is *a personal relationship* with Jesus Christ—seeing how wonderful He is, how glorious He is. We need to come to the place where it can truly be said of us that we love Him because He first loved us. To open up this little book will be like the breaking of Mary's alabaster box of ointment, and I trust that the fragrance of it will fill our lives and spread out to others.

People are being deluded today. They feel that living the Christian life is like following the instructions for putting together a toy. The instructions for a little truck or house will say to take piece "A" and put it down by piece "D" and then take piece "C" and fit it between them. I want to tell you, some of those instructions are really complicated! I know because I buy them for my little grandsons. It almost takes a college degree to be able to put some of those gadgets together.

Some people think that the Christian life is like that. They have the impression that if you can get together a little mixture of psychology, a smattering of common sense, a good dash of salesmanship, and a few verses from the Bible as a sugarcoating over the whole thing, that makes a successful formula for living the Christian life.

My friend, may I say that what we need is a personal relationship with Jesus Christ. We need a hot passion for Him. The Lord is not pleased with this cool, lukewarm condition which exists today in the churches among so-called dedicated Christians. Too many who are called dedicated Christians are actually as cold as a cucumber. Some are even unfriendly and arrogant in their attitudes. What we all need is a real, living, burning passion for the person of the Lord Jesus Christ.

This little book is going to be personal. It is not for the ear of the man who has a personal relationship with the Lord Jesus Christ.

Since the Song of Solomon is a series of scenes in a drama which is not told in chronological sequence, I will make no attempt to outline the book. What we find in this little book is the use of antiphony; that is, one character speaks and another responds. We have many characters: the young bride (she is a Shulamite), the daughters of Jerusalem, the bridegroom, and the Shulamite's family. In the family there is the father (who is dead), the mother, two daughters, and two or more sons.

One interpretation of the story given in the Song of Solomon came out of the German rationalistic schools of the nineteenth century. (It was from these schools that liberalism first crept into the church. Actually, liberalism was and is simply unbelief.) These people tried to interpret the story so that the Shulamite girl was kidnapped by Solomon; at first she did not want to go with him, and then finally she did.

To a child of God who sees in this book the wonderful relationship between Christ and the church, such an interpretation is repugnant. Men like Rutherford, McCheyne, and Moody—this was their favorite book—could not accept this kidnapping interpretation. Neither could the late Dr. Harry Ironside. So he got down on his knees and asked God for an interpretation. Much of what I am going to pass on to you is based on Dr. Ironside's interpretation.

The setting of the drama is the palace in Jerusalem, and some of the scenes are flashbacks to a previous time. There is a reminder here of the Greek drama in which a chorus talks back and forth to the protagonists of the play. The daughters of Jerusalem carry along the tempo of the story. These dialogues are evidently to be sung. Several lovely scenes are introduced at Jerusalem which find a counterpart in the church.

The Shulamite girl says, "Look not upon me, because I am black, because the sun hath looked upon me: my mother's children were angry with me; they made me the keeper of the vineyards; but mine own vineyard have I not kept" (Song 1:6). The elder daughter of this poor Shulamite family is a sort of a Cinderella, and she has been forced to keep the vineyard. She is darkened with sunburn from working out in the vineyard. Apparently this family lived in the hill country of Ephraim, and they were tenant farmers. We would call them croppers or hillbillies. We get this picture from a verse in the last chapter: "Solomon had a vineyard at Baal-hamon; he let out the vineyard unto keepers; every one for the fruit thereof was to bring a thousand pieces of silver" (Song 8:11).

I think that is the setting where the first scene takes place. The girl is sunburned and she feels disgraced. In that day a sunburn meant you were a hardworking girl. The women in the court wanted to keep their skin as fair as they possibly could. It was exactly the opposite of our situation here in California. Here the young girls go down to the beach and lie out in the sun all day in order to get a suntan. Today, it's not a disgrace to have a suntan; in fact, it is a disgrace if you don't have one!

Not only was this girl sunburned from working out in the vineyard, but she says that she was unable to keep her own vineyard. That means she hadn't been to the beauty parlor. Apparently she was a naturally beautiful girl, but she hadn't been able to enhance her beauty or groom herself.

She was an outdoor girl, a hardworking girl. Apparently her brothers also made her watch the sheep. "If thou know not, O thou fairest among women, go thy way forth by the footsteps of the flock, and feed thy kids beside the shepherds' tents" (Song 1:8). So she worked in the vineyards and also had to herd the sheep.

The place where she worked was along a caravan route there in the hill country. Perhaps some of you have traveled in that land, and you know how rugged it is. A tour bus goes up through there today, and the tourists take a trip into that part of the country. I have been through that rugged territory twice, and I have pictures of some Arab girls working in the fields. I think that is exactly the way it was with the Shulamite girl.

When she would look up from her work, she would see the caravans that passed by going between Jerusalem and Damascus. We see her reaction: "Who is this that cometh out of the wilderness like pillars of smoke, perfumed with myrrh and frankincense, with all powders of the merchant?" (Song 3:6). She would see the caravans of merchants and also the caravans that carried beautiful ladies of the court. They were the ones who didn't have a sunburn. They had a canopy over them as they traveled on camels or on elephants. The girl would see the beautiful jewels and the satins. She never had anything like that, and she would dream about it, you know.

She also would smell the frankincense and the myrrh as the caravans passed by. We shall see how this is a wonderful picture of the Lord Jesus both in His birth and in His death. They brought Him myrrh as a gift when He was born; when He was dead, they brought myrrh to put on His body. There are wonderful spiritual pictures here, truths that will draw us to the person of Christ.

One day while the girl was tending her sheep, a handsome shepherd appeared. He fell in love with her. I must run ahead enough to tell you it is a picture of Christ and the church. This is what he said to her, "As the lily among thorns, so is my love among the daughters" (Song 2:2). Again, he says, "Behold, thou art fair, my love; behold, thou art fair; thou hast doves' eyes within thy locks: thy hair is as a flock of goats, that appear from mount Gilead" (Song 4:1). This is beautiful poetic language. It is a picture of the love of Christ for the church. Christ loved the church and gave Himself for it.

Finally she gave her heart to the shepherd: "As the apple tree among the trees of the wood, so is my beloved among the sons. I sat down under his shadow with great delight, and his fruit was sweet to my taste" (Song 2:3).

Remember that the word *love* is used when it is speaking of the bride, and *beloved* is the word that refers to the bridegroom.

The Lord Jesus has given us an invitation: "Come unto me, all ye that labour and are heavy laden, and I will [rest you]" (Matt. 11:28). Do you know what it is to rest in Jesus Christ? Is He a reality to you? Do you *rest* in Him? How wonderful this relationship can become to you! I am not talking about religion or about an organization. I am talking about a personal relationship, a love relationship with Jesus Christ.

After she gave her heart to him, they were madly in love. There is nothing quite like marital love such as they experienced. "My beloved is mine, and I am his: he feedeth among the liles" (Song 2:16). How wonderful! They had that wonderful, personal relationship.

Apparently he took her to dinner one time as he traveled through the country. (All she knew of him was that he was a shepherd, but evidently a very prominent one.) "He brought me to the banqueting house, and his banner over me was love" (Song 2:4).

He was a most peculiar shepherd. He didn't have any sheep that she could see. She asked him about his sheep: "Tell me, O thou whom my soul loveth, where thou feedest, where thou makest thy flock to rest at noon . . . ?" (Song 1:7). Where are his sheep? He is an unusual shepherd.

Then one day he announced that he was going away but that he would return. This is an obvious parallel to the words of the Lord Jesus: "Let not your heart be troubled: ye believe in God, believe also in me. In my Father's house are many mansions: if it were not so, I would have told you. I go to prepare a place for you. And if I go and prepare a place for you, I will come again, and receive you unto myself; that where I am, there ye may be also" (John 14:1–3).

The days passed and she waited. Finally, her family and friends began to ridicule her. They said, "You are just a simple, country girl taken in by him." This is exactly what Peter said would happen in our time: "Knowing this first, that there shall come in the last days scoffers, walking after their own lusts, And saying, Where is the promise of his coming? for since the fathers fell asleep, all things continue as they were from the beginning of the creation" (2 Pet. 3:3–4).

Yet she trusted him. She loved him. She *dreamed* of him: "By night on my bed I sought him whom my soul loveth: I sought him, but I found him not" (Song 3:1). Now let me ask you a very personal question. Do you really miss Christ? Do you long for Him?

One night she lay restlessly upon her couch when she noticed a fragrance in the room. In that day it was a custom that a lover would put some myrrh or frankincense in the opening to the door handle. She smelled the perfume and went to the door. "I rose up to open to my beloved; and my hands dropped with myrrh, and my fingers with sweet smelling myrrh, upon the handles of the lock" (Song 5:5). She knew that he had been there. She knew that he really hadn't forgotten.

Are there evidences of the fragrance and the perfume of Christ in your life today? Oh, my friend, don't ever be satisfied with religious gimmicks. Why not get right down to where the rubber meets the road? What does Christ mean to you right now? Is the fragrance of Christ in your life today?

Now she knew that her lover was near. The Lord Jesus said, ". . . Lo, I am with you alway, even unto the end of the world" (Matt. 28:20). Paul could say while he was in prison that the Lord stood by him. The Lord Jesus has promised, ". . . I will never leave thee, nor forsake thee" (Heb. 13:5).

One day she is in the vineyard working with the vines. "Take us the foxes, the little foxes, that spoil the vines: for our vines have tender grapes" (Song 2:15). She is lifting up the vines so that the little foxes cannot get to the grapes. In that land, they raise the grapes right down on the ground. They do not string them up as we do in this country. So she is lifting up the vines and putting a rock under them so that the little foxes will not get to the grapes.

While she is doing this, down the road there comes a pillar of smoke. "Who is this that cometh out of the wilderness like pillars of smoke, perfumed with myrrh and frankincense, with all powders of the merchant?" (Song 3:6). The cry is passed along, "Behold, king Solomon is coming!" But she is busy, and she doesn't know king Solomon. Then someone comes to her excitedly and says to her, "Oh, king Solomon is asking for you!" And she says, "Asking for me? I don't know king Solomon. I've never met him, why would he ask for me?"

"The voice of my beloved! behold, he cometh leaping upon the mountains, skipping upon the hills. My beloved is like a roe or a young hart: behold, he standeth behind our wall, he looketh forth at the windows, shewing himself through the lattice. My beloved spake, and said unto me, Rise up, my love, my fair one, and come away" (Song 2:8–10). And so she is brought into the presence of king Solomon. Do you know who king Solomon is? Why, he is her shepherd, and he has come for her.

This is the promise of the Lord Jesus: "My sheep hear my voice, and I know them, and they follow me: And I give unto them eternal life; and they shall never perish, neither shall any man pluck them out of my hand" (John 10:27–28). Paul writes, "For the Lord himself shall descend from heaven with a shout, with the voice of the archangel, and with the trump of God: and the dead in Christ shall rise first: Then we which are alive and remain shall be caught up together with them in the clouds, to meet the Lord in the air: and so shall we ever be with the Lord" (1 Thess. 4:16–17). The Lord Jesus has promised that He is coming again for us. "For, lo, the winter is past, the rain is over and gone; The flowers appear on the earth; the time of the singing of birds is come, and the voice of the turtle is heard in our land; The fig tree putteth forth her green figs, and the vines with the tender grape give a good smell. Arise, my love, my fair one, and come away" (Song 2:11–13). One of these days He is going to call us out of this world.

By the way, how much are you involved in the world? I have a feeling there are some people who are so satisfied down here, who are doing so well in this affluent society, that if He should come for them, they would go crying all the way to heaven because they have so much here in this life. He says to her, "Arise, my love, my fair one, and come away. O my dove, that art in the clefts of the rock." That is where the Lord puts us—in the cleft of the rock until the storm passes. "In the secret places of the stairs, let me see thy countenance, let me hear thy voice; for sweet is thy voice, and thy countenance is comely" (Song 2:13–14). What a glorious thing!

"He brought me to the banqueting house, and his banner over me was love" (Song 2:4). Salvation is a love affair—we love Him because He first loved us. That is the story that this little book is telling.

# CHAPTER 1

It is important for you to read the beautiful story of this book before you come to the text. I have given this in some detail in the introduction.

There are five canticles or brief songs in the book. They depict the experience and the story of a country girl, a Shulamite, up in the hill country. A shepherd came one day, and she fell in love with him, and he fell in love with her. He left her but promised to return. He didn't return as soon as she had expected. One day it was announced that king Solomon had arrived and wanted to see her. She couldn't believe it. When she was brought into his presence, she recognized that he was her shepherd-lover.

Some interpreters feel that this is a connected story told in sequence. I personally do not hold that view. I think the scene shifts, and there are flashbacks to earlier times. However, the primary concern for us in our study is the application of this book to you and me as believers. It is a picture of the beautiful love relationship between the believer and the Lord Jesus Christ.

**The song of songs, which is Solomon's [Song 1:1].**

I suppose one could liken this book to a piece of folk music, or more likely to an opera. These canticles are put together to give us a glorious, wonderful story. This is one of the methods God used in speaking to His people. It rebukes asceticism, but it also condemns lust and unfaithfulness to the marriage vow. This is no soap opera. It is not a cheap play in which the hero is a neurotic, the heroine is erotic, and the plot is tommyrotic. Rather, it is a beautiful song of marital love.

## HIS KISS

In this first song, we find the bride and the bridegroom together in a wonderful relationship.

**Let him kiss me with the kisses of his mouth: for thy love is better than wine [Song 1:2].**

The kiss in that day was the pledge of peace, a token of peace. Solomon's very name means peace. He was a prince of peace and he ruled in Jerusalem, the city of peace. The Shulamite girl is the daughter of peace.

The kiss indicates the existence of a very personal, close relationship, such as the Lord Jesus has with His own. He is able to communicate His message personally to you and me through the Word of God. That is why there needs to be a return to a study of the Word of God—more than just learning the mechanics of the Bible, or even memorizing the Word, but a personal relationship with Him so that He can speak through His Word to our hearts. "Let him kiss me with the kisses of his mouth." He has spoken peace to us, you see. He alone can speak peace to the human heart.

In the Old Testament we have seen types of Christ. A. Moody Stuart has written: "Moses and the prophets have come, Aaron and the priests have come, and last of all, David and the kings have come; but let Him now come himself, the true prophet, priest, and king, of all his people." And Bernard, one who had drawn very close to Christ, commented: "I hear not Moses for he is slow of speech, the lips of Isaiah are unclean, Jeremiah cannot speak because he is a child, and all the prophets are dumb; Himself, himself of whom they speak, let him speak" (*The Song of Songs: An Exposition of the Song of Solomon,* p. 95).

The one who has ears to hear and has heard Him speak peace—peace through the blood of His cross by forgiveness of sin—can take the next step. If you have been reconciled to God by redemption in Christ, He entreats the kiss of the solemn, nuptial contract. It is the kiss which seals the marriage vow between Christ and the believer.

We find this same custom in our marriage ceremonies today. When I perform a marriage ceremony and both couples have said "I will" and "I do," I say, "Lift the bride's veil and give the marriage kiss." The kiss is a solemn thing; it seals the marriage covenant.

In redemption, the Lord Jesus not only gives us deliverance, but He also gives us freedom. "If the Son therefore shall make you free, ye shall be free indeed" (John 8:36). What kind of freedom is that? It is the freedom now to come to Him and to say, "I present my body as a living sacrifice to You" (see Rom. 12:1). It is the freedom of dedication, which brings us into a personal relationship with Jesus Christ, our Savior.

Are you such a child of God? Are you a trembling soul who is afraid to lay hold of His grace? He *wants* you to appropriate it for yourself. In Ephesians we are told that He is rich in mercy and He is rich in grace, and He wants to share with us the riches of His glory.

I don't know how you feel about this, but I know that I need His mercy, and I need His grace. His invitation is, "Come unto me, all ye that labour and are heavy laden, and I will give you rest" (Matt. 11:28). This is a real rest. It is not rest for just one day on the Sabbath. This is a rest for the seven days of the week. It is resting in His finished redemption. Then He says, "Take my yoke upon you, and learn of me; for I am meek and lowly in heart: and ye shall find rest unto your souls. For my yoke is easy, and my burden is light" (Matt. 11:29–30). Being yoked up with Him is a wonderful, glorious relationship. And He is the One who carries the load for you.

Erskine expressed it poetically:

> His mouth the joy of heaven reveals;
> His kisses from above,
> Are pardons, promises, and seals
> Of everlasting love.

## HIS LOVE

"For thy love is better than wine." In that day wine typified the highest of the luxuries this earth offered. It was the champagne dinner, which included everything from soup to nuts. It speaks of that which brings the highest joy to the heart. Paul wrote, "And be not drunk with wine, wherein is excess; but be filled with the Spirit" (Eph. 5:18). Oh, to be filled with the Holy Spirit so that we might experience that excitement, that exhilaration, that ecstasy of belonging to Christ and of having fellowship with Him!

Friend, I am talking about something that neither you nor I know very much about, do we? We play at church. We talk about being dedicated Christians simply because we are as busy as termites, and often have the same effect. We need to come to that attitude of which Peter wrote: "Whom having not seen, ye love; in whom, though now ye see him not, yet believing, ye rejoice with joy unspeakable and full of glory" (1 Pet. 1:8).

Habakkuk stated it like this: "Although the fig tree shall not blossom, neither shall fruit be in the vines; the labour of the olive shall fail, and the fields shall yield no meat; the flock shall be cut off from the fold, and there shall be no herd in the stalls: Yet I will rejoice in the Lord, I will joy in the God of my salvation" (Hab. 3:17–18). Have you arrived at that place? No wonder it says, "Thy love is better than wine."

I do not mean to be irreverent, but do you get a kick out of life? Well, this is the way to get it. Wine is excess and may lead you to alcoholism. Wine will give a temporary lift, I grant you, but it will let you down. My friend, allow the Spirit of God to come into your life. He will shed abroad in your heart the love of God. That is one reason we need the Holy Spirit.

**Because of the savour of thy good ointments thy name is as ointment poured forth, therefore do the virgins love thee [Song 1:3].**

The "ointment" is the perfume. When He began His life on earth, myrrh was brought to be put on His body. There was a fragrance in His entire life on earth from His birth to His death. Oh, the fragrance of His love for us when He died upon the cross!

## HIS DRAWING POWER

**Draw me, we will run after thee: the king hath brought me into his chambers: we will be glad and rejoice in thee, we will remember thy love more than wine: the upright love thee [Song 1:4].**

This is a wonderful passage of Scripture. It is the expression of one who is in love with Him, who desires a close fellowship with Him. But then comes the awareness that we can't reach that state; we cannot attain to it because it is too high for us. That is the position from which we say, "Draw me."

Bonar expressed his love in these lines:

> I love the name of Jesus,
> Immanuel, Christ the Lord,
> Like fragrance on the breezes,
> His name abroad is poured.

What does the name of Jesus mean to you? If you know that you have never experienced that wonderful relationship, then listen to the bride, and give her response, "Draw me." If you are a child of God, then say, "Draw me." Let Him lift you up and bring you to this place which you cannot reach yourself. Recognize that in yourself you cannot rise to that level. Francis Quarles has expressed this thought beautifully:

> But like a block beneath whose burden lies
> That undiscovered worm that never dies,
> I have no will to rouse, I have no power to rise.
> For can the water-buried axe implore
> A hand to raise it, or itself restore,
> And from her sandy deeps approach the dry-foot
> shore?
> So hard's the task for sinful flesh and blood,

To lend the smallest help to what is good;
My God, I cannot move the least degree.
Ah! if but only those who active be,
None should thy glory see, they glory none should see.
Lord, as I am, I have no power at all
To hear thy voice, or echo to thy call.

Give me the power to will, the will to do;
O raise me up, and I will strive to go:
Draw me, O draw me with thy treble-twist;
That have no power, but merely to resist;
O lend me strength to do, and then command thy list.

God tells us that His power is available to us. He says that His strength is made perfect in our weakness. He will answer the heart cry, "Draw me," Lord. There is an excitement and an ecstasy of being brought into the presence of Christ by the Spirit of God. He can make Christ real to us.

"No man can come to me, except the Father which hath sent me draw him . . ." (John 6:44). The Lord Jesus said to His own, "Ye have not chosen me, but I have chosen you . . ." (John 15:16)—"I am the One who went after you." We did not seek after God; God sought after us. He is still seeking us today. We can only rouse ourselves to say, Lord, "draw me." We need the Spirit of God to give to us the Water of Life. If we will drink of that Water of Life, we will have rivers of living water gushing up within us and flowing out from us.

"We will run after thee." The idea here is not that we ask to be drawn because we are lazy and indifferent, but we are helpless. We have the desire—the spirit is willing, but the flesh is weak. We want to run after Him, but He will have to give us the legs to do it. He must give us that enablement, that divine enablement. He must draw us. "Wherefore . . . let us run with patience the race that is set before us, Looking unto Jesus the author and finisher of our faith . . ." (Heb. 12:1–2). "But they that wait upon the LORD shall renew their strength; they shall mount up with wings as eagles; they shall run, and not be weary; and they shall walk, and not faint" (Isa. 40:31).

## HIS CHAMBERS

So when we cry. "Draw me, we will run after thee," He responds—"The king hath brought me into his chambers." The chamber is the secret of His presence, His pavilion, like the Holy of Holies within the sanctuary. It is the secret place away from the crowd. It is the place in the cleft of the rock which He has made for us, where He can cover us with His hand and commune with us. It is like Christ's invitation: "Behold, I stand at the door, and knock: if any man hear my voice, and open the door, I will come in to him, and will sup with him, and he with me" (Rev. 3:20). Oh, what a privilege to fellowship with Him!

Yet we withdraw and cry out with Isaiah, ". . . Woe is me! for I am undone; because I am a man of unclean lips, and I dwell in the midst of a people of unclean lips: for mine eyes have seen the King, the LORD of hosts" (Isa. 6:5). But "the king hath brought me into his chambers"—He is the One who has provided a redemption. He is the One who took the coals from the altar and touched our lips. He is the One who made the supreme sacrifice.

"We will be glad and rejoice in thee." We need more joy in our churches, and we need more joy in our lives. Jesus said, ". . . I am come that they might have life, and that they might have it more *abundantly*" (John 10:10, italics mine). And John wrote, ". . . These things write we unto you, that your *joy* may be full" (1 John 1:4, italics mine). The Lord means for us to live life to the hilt.

Oh, let's quit playing church, and let's quit saying, "I belong to a certain group, and I have had an *experience*." The point is, is Christ close to you *today*? "The king hath brought me into his chambers: we will be glad and rejoice in thee, we will remember thy love more than wine: the upright love thee."

At this moment there are probably millions of people across the country who are crawling up onto a bar stool. Well, if I were in their situation, I'd crawl up there too. They need something to face life. Many a man feels he needs that drink in order to face his business. Many a person needs that drink in order to face a lonely evening. Life is too much for them. It is too complicated. May I say to you, if you are a child of God, you can always know that God loves you. The love of

God is shed abroad in our hearts by the Holy Spirit who has been given to us. He wants to make His love real to us. He wants to manifest His love to us. That is a lot better than crawling up onto a bar stool. ". . . Be not drunk with wine, wherein is excess; but be filled with the Spirit" (Eph. 5:18).

If we would read on in Ephesians 5, we would find the next verse going on to say, "Speaking to yourselves in psalms and hymns and spiritual songs, singing and making melody in your heart to the Lord" (Eph. 5:19). I have always been glad that Paul didn't write, "Singing to yourselves," because I can't sing. But I can speak it. I can say it. It wouldn't hurt for you to say it either. In fact, it would be good to hear a "Praise the Lord" from all of us believers. Oh, we need to praise the Lord in this day. "We will be glad and rejoice in thee, we will remember thy love more than wine."

"The upright love thee." Who are the upright? They are those who belong to Him. They are those who have said to Him, "Draw me." He has placed them on their feet, and they are to run the race of life, looking unto Jesus, the author and finisher of their faith.

The Christian life is a love affair. We love Him because He first loved us. He loved us enough to give Himself for us. Now He says to us, "I want your love." That seals it. If you don't love Him, then don't go on pretending. Be honest and chuck the whole thing. It is all meaningless if you do not love Him.

Now listen to the believer's loving response, as we find it in Psalm 64: "O God, thou art my God; early will I seek thee: my soul thirsteth for thee, my flesh longeth for thee in a dry and thirsty land, where no water is" (Ps. 63:1). My friend, are you thirsty for God? The Lord Jesus said, ". . . If any man thirst, let him come unto me, and drink" (John 7:37).

"To see thy power and thy glory, so as I have seen thee in the sanctuary" (Ps. 63:2)—this is the bride's secret place of communion.

"Because thy lovingkindness is better than life, my lips shall praise thee. Thus will I bless thee while I live: I will lift up my hands in thy name. My soul shall be satisfied as with marrow and fatness; and my mouth shall praise thee with joyful lips" (Ps. 63:3–5). Oh, friend, let's get our lips busy praising Him!

"Because thou hast been my help, therefore in the shadow of thy wings will I rejoice" (Ps. 63:7). You remember that the Lord Jesus said that He wanted to gather the people of Jerusalem under His wings like a hen gathers her chicks (see Matt. 23:37). This gives to us a picture of His love and the great desire to protect the helpless ones from harm.

"My soul followeth hard after thee: thy right hand upholdeth me. But those that seek my soul, to destroy it, shall go into the lower parts of the earth. They shall fall by the sword: they shall be a portion for foxes. But the king shall rejoice in God; every one that sweareth by him shall glory: but the mouth of them that speak lies shall be stopped" (Ps. 63:8–11). What a glorious picture of a believer's devotion to Christ!

## THE SUNBURNED SLAVE GIRL

**I am black, but comely, O ye daughters of Jerusalem, as the tents of Kedar, as the curtains of Solomon.**

**Look not upon me, because I am black, because the sun hath looked upon me: my mother's children were angry with me; they made me the keeper of the vineyards; but mine own vineyard have I not kept [Song 1:5–6].**

"The tents of Kedar" were made of the skin of the black sheep and the black goats. In that land even today one can see many of these nomad people who have black tents.

When the bride says here that she is black, she is not referring to her race. She was a Jewish girl from the area of Shunem. She explains the blackness herself. Her family were tenant farmers on one of the vineyards owned by Solomon, and they made her work out in the vineyard. She is sunburned—"I am black, because the sun hath looked upon me." She is black, but she is beautiful. Black is beautiful, we hear today. It certainly can be. Black is beautiful when the heart is right with the Lord. The pigment of the skin is of no importance whatever. The condition of the heart is the important matter.

It is interesting that most of the rays of the sun do not bother our skin. It is the ultraviolet segment of the sun's rays that burns our skin. Those rays can come through clouds, so that we can get sunburned on cloudy days even when we are unaware of it. Since I have had cancer, my doctor warns me about sunlight. He tells me to keep my head covered, even on the cloudy days. He warns me against going out into the sunlight. The ultraviolet rays can burn, and they can cause cancer.

A great many people think they can come into the light to the holy presence of God without a covering. I tell you, no one can come into the holy presence of God without the covering of the righteousness of Christ. That is our protection—which is another meaning of being covered with His wings. You and I need to be clothed in the righteousness of Christ to come into the presence of God.

Let's get back to our girl who is blackened with sunburn. She has been working outside because her mother's children were angry with her, and they made her keep the vineyards. Then she says, "But mine own vineyard have I not kept." This is the bride's portrait of herself. She has some natural beauty, but she has nothing to commend her because she hasn't been able to take care of herself. She has had no time to go to the beauty parlor. She hasn't been able to have her hair styled. She hasn't been able to get a facial. She hasn't been able to get whatever it would take to enhance her beauty. That has been neglected because she has been made to work so hard.

Mankind is not beautiful in the presence of God. Sometimes we tend to think that the reason God is interested in us is because we are such nice, sweet little children. Actually we are ugly; we are sunburned. We are not attractive to Him as we are, but He says that He is going to make us His beautiful bride. That is the wonderful picture given to us in Ephesians 5. The example given to husbands is the love of Christ for the church. "Husbands, love your wives, even as Christ also loved the church, and gave himself for it; That he might sanctify and cleanse it with the washing of water by the word, That he might present it to himself a glorious church, not having spot, or wrinkle, or any such thing; but that it should be holy and without blemish" (Eph. 5:25–27). You see, Christ is taking us to the beauty parlor. He will fashion us into His bride, without spot or wrinkle, holy and without blemish!

## THE PASTURE

Now the story moves on. The Shulamite speaks to the shepherd whom she has just met.

> **Tell me, O thou whom my soul loveth, where thou feedest, where thou makest thy flock to rest at noon: for why should I be as one that turneth aside by the flocks of thy companions? [Song 1:7].**

He seemed to be an unusual shepherd in that he didn't have any sheep that she could see. So she raised a question concerning his sheep. The shepherd seemed to be evasive. Now let's look beneath the surface and see something very precious.

The Lord Jesus said, "I am the good shepherd, and know my sheep, and am known of mine. . . . And other sheep I have, which are not of this fold: them also I must bring, and they shall hear my voice; and there shall be one fold, and one shepherd" (John 10:14, 16). We all tend to raise questions, as the Shulamite girl asked the shepherd, about "the other sheep," the heathen. Are they lost? We want to know about the doctrine of election. We want to know about this one or that one—is he saved, or isn't he saved? We tend to pass judgment on those who are around us. Instead of questioning another's position in Christ, we need to make sure that *we* are His sheep. That is our direct concern.

The shepherd answers her.

> **If thou know not, O thou fairest among women, go thy way forth by the footsteps of the flock, and feed thy kids beside the shepherds' tents [Song 1:8].**

And this would be the answer of the Lord Jesus to us.

"Feed thy kids"—the little lambs need to be fed, and all of us, my friend, come under that classification. Peter put it this way, "As newborn babes, desire the sincere milk of the word, that ye may grow thereby" (1 Pet. 2:2).

"Feed thy kids beside the shepherds' tents." Believers need to feed themselves beside the shepherds' tents because that is the place where the grass would be unusually green. Of course it is the Word of God on which we are to feed. We cannot feed others and tell them about the joy of the Word of God unless it is a joy to us. Herbert puts it this way:

> My soul's a shepherd too, a flock it feeds
> Of thoughts and words and deeds;
> The pasture is thy word, the streams thy grace,
> Enriching all the place.

We need to feed upon the Word of God, then we need to get the Word out to others, you see. The Bride of Christ, who is to be presented to Him in the future, is to get the Word of God out today. As the body of believers, we are failing to do this.

"If thou know not, O thou fairest among women"—there are many things for which we do not have the answer. When I was a young preacher, I tried to get the answer to everything. I was given some good advice: "Don't let what you don't know disturb what you do know!" Do you know that Christ died for your sins? Do you know that you are trusting in Him? Are you resting upon Him? You can say, ". . . I know that my redeemer liveth . . ." (Job 19:25). You can say, ". . . I know whom I have believed . . ." (2 Tim. 1:12)—Paul could say that, but I don't find Paul saying that he knew all about the doctrine of election. So let's not permit what we don't know to disturb what we do know. That is what the shepherd is saying to this girl. Don't worry about what you don't know. Just be sure to feed your sheep. That is your responsibility.

There is a bedridden lady in Ohio who hears our radio broadcasts. She contacts about one thousand people each month, and she asks them to listen to the Bible being taught by radio. She is a real missionary! Now I am sure that she is puzzled by many things and has questions to ask about things she doesn't know, but so far I have never received a letter from her with a question in it. She isn't spending her time asking questions. She is spending her time getting out the Word of God. That is exactly what the shepherd tells the girl. He says, "You don't need to know about all these other sheep. You just feed your sheep." Be sure you get the Word of God to them.

## THE BRIDE'S ADORNING

The shepherd uses a comparison as he goes on to say:

> I have compared thee, O my love, to a company of horses in Paraoh's chariots [Song 1:9].

As I have mentioned before, when the word *love* is used, it is the bridegroom speaking to the bride. When the person is addressed as *beloved*, it is the bride who is speaking to the bridegroom.

"I have compared thee, O my love, to a company of horses in Pharaoh's chariots." When Moses and the children of Israel came to the Red Sea in their flight from Egypt, they found that any retreat was blocked by Pharaoh's chariots which were rapidly approaching. It was a fearsome army with horses and chariots and banners flying above the chariots. It was an overwhelming sight. The bridegroom is saying that he is overwhelmed by the beauty of this country, hillbilly girl. She has none of the graces of the court. She has never been to a beauty parlor. She really has never taken care of herself. But she has a striking natural beauty.

He goes on to describe the things that he notices.

> Thy cheeks are comely with rows of jewels, thy neck with chains of gold.

> We will make thee borders of gold with studs of silver [Song 1:10–11].

"Thy cheeks are comely." Her neck is beautiful. How lovely this is and how intimate. He says that he intends to cover her with jewelry. He sees her cheeks comely with jewels, her neck with chains of gold. He speaks of the parts of the body that appeal in a love affair. I am sure there are many of you ladies who noticed the eyelashes of your husband—of all things! You noticed his physique. You husbands noticed the cheeks and the eyes of your wife, and even the little ears, like shells—and all that sort of thing. He is speaking of this girl who will be his bride.

Now in the spiritual sense, the bride is the church, and the bridegroom is the Lord Jesus Christ. Does He find any beauty in the church? Friend, He found all of us lost sinners. The Shulamite girl had a natural beauty even though it had been neglected, but we don't even have that. There is nothing about us that could be appealing to Christ. We bring nothing to Him; He provides everything for us.

The same picture can be applied to Israel. When He came down to deliver the children of Israel, He didn't say, "I'm going to free you because you're such a superior people, superior to the Egyptians." They weren't. Actually, they were small and inferior. Neither did He say, "You have been so faithful to Me." They had been unfaithful—completely faithless, living in idolatry. They had deserted God. They had turned their backs upon God and were engaged in gross immorality. Then what was it that appealed to God? Why did He waste His time with them? The answer is given by God to Moses: ". . . I have heard their groaning" (Acts 7:34). *That* appealed to God. The answer lies totally in His love and grace. It was the lost condition that caused Him to provide a salvation for Israel. And He said that He remembered His covenant with Abraham, Isaac, and Jacob. God is faithful to His Word. When He says he will do a thing, He intends to make that promise good.

And it was our wretched, lost condition that caused Him to provide a salvation for us, for the church. God tells us that we will be saved if we will do nothing more than put our trust in Christ!

"We will make thee borders of gold with studs of silver"—this is a picture of what our heavenly Bridegroom will do for believers. The passage in Ephesians 5 makes this so very clear. Christ loved the church and gave Himself for the church. He did it so that He might sanctify and cleanse the church with the washing of water by the Word. That is a real miracle soap, by the way. He did this so that He might present the church of Himself, a glorious church without a spot or a wrinkle but holy—set apart for Him—and without blemish. What has happened to the church? He has redeemed us. He has paid the price for us. He has subtracted our sins and has added His righteousness. We are covered with the righteousness of Christ, we stand complete in Him, accepted in the Beloved.

## FEASTING AT THE ROUND TABLE

**While the king sitteth at his table, my spikenard sendeth forth the smell thereof [Song 1:12].**

Some have translated this, "While the king is on his circuit." They interpret it to mean while he is out going through the kingdom. Others have translated this, "While the king is at his banquet," which I think is probably the best translation that could be given. Very literally it is, "While the king sitteth at his round table"—that is the circuit. It is actually a round table where he either sits or reclines with his guests around the banquet table.

The translation is important because this verse carries with it a deeper spiritual meaning. The bridegroom brings in all of His invited guests to the banquet table. We can go down through history and mark those who have accepted the invitation to the banquet of the Bridegroom. When He was born, the shepherds came down from the hilltops to see Him in the stable. Then wise men came out of the East to present Him with gifts of gold and frankincense and myrrh. John Milton expressed it like this:

> See how from far upon the Eastern road,
> The star-led wizards haste with odours sweet;
> O run, prevent them with thy humble ode,
> And lay it lowly at his blessed feet;
> Have thou the honor first thy Lord to greet.

David had the round table in mind when he wrote, "Thou preparest a table before me in the presence of mine enemies: thou anointest my head with oil; my cup runneth over" (Ps. 23:5).

A towheaded boy in southern Oklahoma heard the invitation and, thank God, accepted it. I have been sitting at His table for a long, long time. Are you sitting at that round table? You have an invitation to come. Jesus says to you, "Behold, I stand at the door, and knock: if any man hear my voice, and open the door, I will come in to him, and will sup with him, and he with me" (Rev. 3:20). Say, why don't you come and sit at the round table? Sir Lancelot may have had the privilege of sitting at King Arthur's round table, but that was nothing compared to Christ's round table!

"While the king sitteth at his table, my spikenard sendeth forth the smell thereof." The spikenard is the fragrance of Christ's life—how wonderful it is! This same fragrance should be in our lives by association with Him. Sitting at His table will do this for us. The ordinance of the Lord's Supper is a very important service if it is a time of real communion with Him. If it is merely a form and ritual to you, forget it—it is of no value.

I received a letter from a lady in Miami who wrote, "I had never heard anyone say that we should tell the Lord Jesus we love Him. I had never said it, but I have loved Him. Ever since I heard you say that we should tell Him, at morning, noon, and night (I have been making up for lost time), I tell Him that I love Him." Then she added, "The Word of God has taken on a new color—a new meaning." How wonderful! We need the fragrance of Christ in our lives.

### THE BUNDLE OF MYRRH IN THE BOSOM

Now the bride makes a statement which is quite intimate—but don't be afraid of it and run from it.

> **A bundle of myrrh is my wellbeloved unto me; he shall lie all night betwixt my breasts [Song 1:13].**

The original permits us to translate this several different ways: "It shall lie all night betwixt my breasts." What is "it"? Well, it is the bundle of myrrh.

For the believer, the bundle of myrrh represents Christ. You recall that one of the gifts the wise men brought to Him was myrrh. When Christ died, Joseph and Nicodemus brought myrrh to put on His body. The myrrh speaks of His entire life from birth to death. My friend, Christ should lie heavy upon your breast and upon your heart at night. When you wake up during the night, what do you think about? Do you begin to worry about the next day? I must confess that I do a lot of that. But it is wonderful to be able to turn that off and to turn to *Him* at night when I'm anxious or worried. We need to follow the admonition in Philippians 4:8: "Finally, brethren [when you get to the end of your rope], whatsoever things are true [that is Christ], whatsoever things are honest [that is also Christ], whatsoever things are just [that is the Lord Jesus], whatsoever things are pure [He is pure], whatsoever things are lovely, whatsoever things are of good report; if there be any virtue, and if there be any praise, *think* on these things" (italics mine). In other words, meditate upon the Lord Jesus Christ.

> A bundle of mellifluous myrrhe,
>   Is my Beloved best
> To me, which I will bind between
>   My breasts, while I do rest
> In silent slumbers.
>           —*Troth-plight Spouse*

A friend of mine said it this way: "When I go to bed at night, the last thing I do is pull up the covers, look up, and say, 'Lord Jesus, I love you.'" Isaac Watts wrote it like this:

> As myrrh new bleeding from the tree,
> Such is a dying Christ to me;
> And while He makes my soul his guest,
> My bosom, Lord, shall be thy rest.

Oh, friend, let's think upon the Lord Jesus Christ. How wonderful He is!

Erskine wrote it this way:

From this enfolded bundle flies
His savor all abroad:
Such complicated sweetness lies
In my Incarnate God.

My Christian friend, you miss so much when you are satisfied with some little course on how to live the Christian life or on going through some little ritual. Oh, to have *Him* as the very object of your life, the One who brings in the excitement, the ecstasy, the fellowship, and the joy. His grace and His love and His mercy are all yours—just open the door. Jesus is knocking right now.

## THE CLUSTER OF CAMPHIRE

The bride continues to speak of her delight in her bridegroom.

**My beloved is unto me as a cluster of camphire in the vineyards of En-gedi [Song 1:14].**

The "camphire" mentioned here is the cypress. In some versions it is translated "henna flowers," and the flowers of the cypress are that color. Scholars have done a great deal of study of different plants mentioned in this book. The cypress is a tree that grows in profusion in Palestine and in Turkey. As I traveled in that area, I was most impressed by the great rows of cypress trees. Here is a statement about the cypress from Kitto, which I would like to pass on to you. The camphire "is now generally agreed to be the Henna of the Arabians. The deep color of the bark, the light green of the foliage, and the softened mixture of white-yellow in the blossoms, present a combination as agreeable to the eye as the odour is to the scent. The flowers grow in dense clusters, the grateful fragrance of which is as much appreciated now as in the time of Solomon. The women take great pleasure in these clusters, hold them in their hand, carry them in their bosom, and keep them in their apartments to perfume the air."

Now notice the comparison of camphor or cypress to the

bridegroom—what a lovely thing it is: "My beloved is unto me as a cluster of camphire in the vineyards of En-gedi."

En-gedi, another place that I have visited, is down by the Dead Sea. It is one of those wonderful oases in the desert because there are springs there. You may recall that the area around En-gedi is a wilderness where David hid from Saul. It is a good hiding place—I don't see how anyone could be found in those barren hills. But at En-gedi many kinds of lovely spices are grown. It is a very interesting spot in the midst of that desolate desert, and the bridegroom is like a cluster of camphor in the vineyards of En-gedi. He is like a row of those stately trees with that lovely fragrance.

Christ as our Beloved is represented here as being full of attractive beauty and an aromatic fragrance. I emphasize the deity of Christ very often, but I wonder sometimes if I give a lopsided view of Him. Have you ever stopped to think how lovely He was in His person? He came and took upon Himself our humanity, and He was in all points tempted as we are, yet without sin. There was no sin in Him. How wonderful He was! There was nothing lopsided about His personality. You may recall that in the Old Testament the meal offering typified the even quality of Christ's personality. It was well-beaten flour—never coarse or lumpy.

Frankly, most of us are lumpy—I don't mean physically, but psychologically. All of us are a little "off" in one way or another. We all have our peculiarities. One man talking to another made the statement, "You know we all have our peculiarities." The man replied, "I don't believe that. I don't think I have any peculiarities." The first man said, "All right. Let me ask you a question. Do you stir your coffee with your right hand or your left hand?" He answered, "I stir it with my right hand." "There," he said triumphantly, "that's your peculiarity. Most people use a spoon!" So, you see, we may not stir our coffee with our hand, but we all have peculiarities. We are lumpy; He was not.

He is the perfect human in His incarnation. He is lovely. He is the bundle of camphor. He is the One of whom John could say with enthusiasm and deep expression, ". . . Behold the Lamb of God, which taketh away the sin of the world" (John1:29). If you will hear Him, your soul shall live. Or, as the psalmist says, "O taste and see that the LORD is good . . ." (Ps. 34:8). The Lord Jesus was a sacrifice—He ". . . hath given himself for us an offering and a sacrifice to God for a sweet-smelling savour" (Eph. 5:2). He typified the burnt offering that ascended up to heaven. It all speaks of the fact that God is completely satisfied with what Jesus did for you and for me. He is satisfied with Jesus. He said, ". . . This is my beloved Son, in whom I am well pleased" (Matt. 3:17). He has never said that about Vernon McGee, and probably He has never said it about you. But He has declared that He is satisfied with Jesus.

Friend, are you satisfied with Jesus? I don't think many people are. If they were, they wouldn't be running here and there over the face of the earth, trying to find satisfaction in something else. People run to hear this thing and that thing, always searching for something that is new. We can even become so engrossed in the mechanics and the details of Bible study that we lose sight of the person of Jesus Christ. How wonderful He is! "My beloved is unto me as a cluster of camphire in the vineyards of En-gedi."

There is another interesting symbol in the "bundle" of camphire. There is a great emphasis in the Scriptures on the oneness of the Lord Jesus Christ. He is the *only* begotten Son of the Father. He is the *one* good Shepherd. He is the *one* true Vine. He is the *one* Light of the world. He is the *one* Servant of the Father. He is the *one* Sacrifice for sin. He is the *one* Way, the *one* Truth, the *one* Life. Yet in His perfect unity there is a fullness that is absolutely inexhaustible. He is also a cluster of fragrant flowers. There is a oneness in Him; but, oh, in Him there is *everything*. Innumerable graces crowd harmoniously together in the Lamb of God. In Him we can find the faith of Abraham, the persuasiveness of Jacob, the meekness of Moses, the zeal of Elijah, the holiness of Job, the love of John. They are all full and perfect in Him. In Him are found truth, righteousness, wisdom, love, pity, friendship, majesty, might, sovereignty, lowliness, patience, faith, zeal, courage, holiness, and all the graces. If I have left out any of His qualities, they ought to be included in this list because He is everything. He is all in all. And He is ours. That is the wonder of it all.

## BEHOLD, THOU ART FAIR

Now after the bride has expressed her adoration of the bridegroom, he says this to her:

**Behold, thou art fair, my love; behold, thou art fair; thou hast doves' eyes [Song 1:15].**

And her instant response is in the following verse: "Behold, thou art fair, my beloved."

She is the one who said, "Look not upon me, because I am black, because the sun hath looked upon me." But he says to her, "Behold, thou art fair, my love; behold, thou art fair."

My friend, we as the bride of Christ have sinned. We can confess with Daniel, "We have sinned, and have committed iniquity, and have done wickedly, and have rebelled, even by departing from thy precepts and from thy judgments" (Dan. 9:5). This is the confession of every person if he is a child of God. But our Lord Jesus intercedes for us: ". . . thine they were, and thou gavest them me; and they have kept thy word" (John 17:6). That is our High Priest pleading for you and me. Because we are in Christ, the Father sees no iniquity in us, as God would not see the iniquity of Jacob or perverseness in Israel and would not permit Balaam to curse them. God went down and dealt with His own people; He wouldn't let them get by with sin. But God would not let a heathen prophet curse Israel. He saw Israel in Christ. That is the way He sees us today. "Behold, thou art fair."

The secret of this beauty is in this: "Thou hast doves' eyes." Doves are common emblems of chastity and constancy. Her eyes are fixed upon the bridegroom, and all her beauty is the reflected beauty of the bridegroom. Jesus said, "The light of the body is the eye: if therefore thine eye be single, thy whole body shall be full of light" (Matt. 6:22)—and also full of beauty. "But if thine eye be evil [or double], thy whole body shall be full of darkness . . ." (Matt. 6:23). A believer who has an eye for anything equally with Christ has no beauty in His sight. Jesus laid it on the line: "He that loveth father or mother more than me is not worthy of me: and he that loveth son or daughter more than me is not worthy of me" (Matt. 10:37). It is important for you to answer this question: Do you have your eye fixed upon the Lord Jesus today?

I hear a great deal about "dedication" as I attend many conferences around the country. Folk are always talking about how dedicated they are and how they want to manifest Christ, but these very people are actually lazy. Their service is slipshod. You see, dedication is not something to *talk* about; dedication to Christ is something you *reveal*. It will be manifested in your life. If your eye is upon Him, then His beauty will be reflected in you.

The bridegroom has told the bride how wonderful she is. Now she turns right around and says the very same thing to him.

> **Behold, thou art fair, my beloved, yea, pleasant: also our bed is green.**
>
> **The beams of our house are cedar, and our rafters of fir [Song 1:16–17].**

The bridegroom is beautiful to those of us who believe. He is altogether lovely. Augustine wrote: "He is fair in heaven, fair in the earth; fair in the virgin's womb [He was that holy thing], fair in the arms of His parents, fair in the miracles, fair in His stripes . . . fair in laying down His life, fair in receiving it again; fair on the cross, fair in the sepulchre." This was the way Augustine, that great saint of God of the past, described the Lord Jesus.

"Yea, pleasant"—the word is the Hebrew *naim,* and it is used to describe the wonderful melodies of the sanctuary: ". . . sing praises unto his name; for it is pleasant" (Ps. 135:3). Christ is pleasant; He is lovely. Why would anyone want to run away from the Lord Jesus! He is so wonderful. The word is also used to describe a chosen earthly friend. David said of his loyal friend, Jonathan, "I am distressed for thee, my brother Jonathan: very pleasant hast thou been unto me . . ." (2 Sam. 1:26).

What can we say of the One who is greater than Jonathan? Can you say that Jesus is pleasant to you? It is sweet to be with Him. He is the One who can bring rest to us. Are you satisfied with Him? God the

Father is satisfied with Him. "Behold, thou art fair, my beloved, yea, pleasant."

"Also our bed is green." The "bed" is the English translation for lack of a better word. It is actually the reclining couch where they sat around the banquet. Especially at the time of a marriage feast the banquet couch would be strewn with flowers and green leaves. I think this would be the meaning of the green "bed" if the setting is in Jerusalem.

However, it may be that this is referring back to the time when they first met and is speaking of the green grass where the sheep were. Maybe they just sat on the grass while the sheep were grazing, and that is where they first got acquainted with each other. It would signify the place of communication.

This reminds us of David's psalm: "He maketh me to lie down in green pastures . . ." (Ps. 23:2). When the sheep lies down in green pastures, he is satisfied. He has eaten enough and is full. It is the answer to Christ's invitation to come to Him and rest. He invites all those who are weary and heavy laden to come to Him. The green pastures are there for us. Christian friend, if you are tired and weary, you can rest in Him.

It has been expressed this way by A. Moody Stuart: "'Heavy laden' and hopeless thou art, seeking peace afar off and passing Him who is near, like Hagar in the desert, with the last drop drained from the now shriveled water-skin, thou art ready to lie down and die. But open thine ears and thou wilt hear one say, 'Come unto Me and I will give you rest'; open thine eyes and thou wilt see the well and the green sward around it; and with a full heart thou wilt answer him, 'Behold Thou art pleasant, also our couch is green.' " What a beautiful picture this is!

Do you remember where He reclined? When He first came to this earth, they put Him in a manger. The last place they laid Him was in the tomb of Joseph. He went to that place so that you and I might sit with Him in green pastures.

# CHAPTER 2

### THE ROSE OF SHARON

**I am the rose of Sharon, and the lily of the valleys [Song 2:1].**

In my printed notes on this verse I have said that here the bride speaks of herself, that she is not boasting, but comparing herself to the lowly and humble flowers of that land. Some of the newer translations indicate that she is the one who is speaking here. Well, I want to say that I no longer believe that this is her voice, but that it is the voice of the bridegroom. If she is the one who is speaking, this is actually a picture of the Lord Jesus Christ and His reflected beauty. "I am the rose of Sharon, and the lily of the valleys" is a statement that none of the sons of men could be making. I believe these are the words of the Lord Jesus, not the words of the bride. Many of the older translators have tried to make it clear that it is the king speaking. In the old English Bibles this is said to be the voice of Christ, the bridegroom. In the French and Italian and Portuguese Bibles this is designated as the voice of Christ. Many of the church fathers applied these words to the Lord Jesus.

These words describe the Lord Jesus. He says, ". . . for I am meek and lowly in heart" (Matt. 11:29). If you put a statement like that on my lips, or your lips, or the lips of the angel Gabriel, it wouldn't be humility at all; it would actually be pride. It is true humility from the lips of the Lord Jesus because He stooped in order that He might become meek and lowly. He came down from heaven's glory, and anything beneath heaven is humility on His part.

So here He says, "I am the rose of Sharon, and the lily of the valleys." These are two very interesting flowers. I suppose that among all the flowers the rose has always been—especially in the East—the one that tops the list. And the rose of Sharon is an unusually beautiful flower. The valley of Sharon is that coast valley that goes all the way from Joppa up to Haifa. I have traveled the length and breadth of it several times. It is beautiful at any season of the year. It is a valley where you can see a great many flowers. I took pictures of them, especially the poppy fields. You have probably heard that the finest citrus fruit in the world is grown in Israel. Sharon is the valley where most of it is grown. The rose grows in profusion in that valley. It is the very beautiful flower that speaks of Him.

I do not think roses originally had thorns. I don't think they were intended to be thorny. But as we know them today, they still have thorns. Even the very beautiful rose reminds us that the earth is under a curse and brings forth thorns and thistles (see Gen. 3:18).

An ancient author wrote: "If the king were set over flowers, it would be the rose that should reign over them, being the ornament of the earth, the splendor of plants, the eye of flowers, the beauty of the field."

Now here is something quite interesting. When Jesus said, ". . . I am the bread of life . . ." (John 6:35), He was saying that He is something that is necessary. Bread is the staff of life. We need it to keep us going. It is a necessity of life. He is that food to the perishing sinner. Thousands have reached up a dying hand, a feeble hand, in faith, and have taken the bread. And they have eaten, and they have lived. Jesus also said, "I am the true vine . . ." (John 15:1). As the true vine, He gives the glorious, wonderful joy of the Lord. The Scripture says, "Give strong drink unto him that is ready to perish, and wine unto those that be of heavy hearts" (Prov. 31:6). Christ gives joy—not the alcoholic beverage, but the real joy of the Lord. However, when He says that He is "the rose of Sharon," He is presenting Himself not as a necessity but as an object of pure admiration and delight to the children of men. What a wonderful human being He was! We need to behold Him and let Him occupy our thoughts. He is the One of truth and honesty and purity and beauty upon whom we are to think.

As He walked along with His disciples through the fields, He said, ". . . Consider the lilies of the field, how they grow; they toil not, neither do they spin" (Matt. 6:28). I think He would say to you and me today, "Consider the Rose of Sharon!" In other words, consider *Him*.

We find this same invitation in Hebrews: "Wherefore, holy brethren, partakers of the heavenly calling, *consider* the Apostle and High Priest of our profession, Christ Jesus" (Heb. 3:1). Consider Jesus Christ.

## THE LILY OF THE VALLEYS

"I am . . .the lily of the valleys." This may be a reference to the valley of Esdraelon. This valley has beautiful flowers in it too. Actually, there is a profusion of flowers in all the valleys—along the coast south of Joppa, in the Jordan valley, around the Sea of Galilee. What is the lily of the valleys? There have been questions as to which flower is meant. Apparently it was the iris. The iris grows wild over there, and one can still see a great many of them. I am of the opinion that it does refer to that humble plant, the iris. He is the beautiful, stately rose and the humble iris. "I am the rose of Sharon, and the lily of the valleys."

**As the lily among the thorns, so is my love among the daughters [Song 2:2].**

Bonar expressed it in this way: "Close by these lilies there grew several of the thorny shrubs of the desert; but above them rose the lily, spreading out its fresh green leaf as a contrast to the dingy verdure of these prickly shrubs—'like the lily among thorns, so is my love among the daughters.'" In other words, among "daughters" (meaning here, the daughters of Jerusalem) the bride stands out as a lily among thorns.

Christ is the lily of the valleys—He is pure, He is lovely, He is beautiful, therefore His bride is a lily also, because she bears the image of His loveliness and reflects it to men. This is what the church is to do today. We are to reveal to a world that is filled with thorns, briars, and thistles, the beauty of Christ.

## THE APPLE TREE IN THE WOOD

Now the bride speaks of her beloved using the "trees of the wood" in her comparison—

**As the apple tree among the trees of the wood, so is my beloved among the sons. I sat down under his shadow with great delight, and his fruit was sweet to my taste [Song 2:3].**

"The apple tree among the trees of the wood" is a picture of Christ. Now you may wonder what kind of tree she is talking about. Actually, apples are not grown in that land. I suppose they could be grown, but they would not be very good. The climate is much as it is here in Southern California. We can grow apples, but they are not very good apples because apples require a colder climate. The "apple" referred to here is actually a *citron* fruit, probably an orange tree. I have three orange trees in my yard here in Pasadena, and they make very good shade trees. They are a tree of beauty, and when they blossom, I sit on my patio and enjoy the fragrance of the orange blossoms in spring. No wonder they are used for weddings! And the luscious fruit which the tree bears is both beautiful and healthful.

There are citrus groves in the valley of Sharon, which are said to produce the finest citrus fruit in the world. It has always grown there. The citrus was transplanted to California years ago; it didn't grow here naturally. But it is native to Palestine. There the green of the citrus groves is beautiful to see.

Notice that she says, "I sat down under his shadow with great delight, and his fruit was sweet to my taste." The orange tree affords thick shade like the ". . . shadow of a great rock in a weary land" (Isa. 32:2) and refreshing fruit. Christ is like this wonderful fruit tree in contrast to the fruitless trees of the woods.

## THE BANQUETING HOUSE

**He brought me to the banqueting house, and his banner over me was love [Song 2:4].**

In this is the story of the Shulamite girl whose heart was won by a shepherd who later came as king Solomon to claim her and who took her back to the palace in Jerusalem. Now he takes her to the banqueting house.

In this there is a beautiful picture of the church which will be the bride of Christ. It also reveals the personal relationship which is possible between the Lord Jesus Christ and each individual believer.

"He brought me to the banqueting house." This probably looks forward to that day of the final banquet which is called the "marriage supper of the Lamb." You and I as believers will be there by the grace of God. That is when full satisfaction will be made. But already He has brought me to the table of salvation, and He has brought me to the table of fellowship with Him. He prepares the table before me, the table of the Word of God, and He tells me to eat and be full. He brings me to a table of good things. How good and gracious He is!

We can go back to the birth of the Lord Jesus and see that already He has brought joy unspeakable to a group of people. There were old Simeon and Anna back in the temple who were waiting for Him. They had great hope that He would come during their lifetime. One day Joseph and Mary brought the little boy Jesus into the temple. My, that day the temple became a banqueting house for those two old people who had looked for the salvation of the Lord.

Even before that, God had brought Joseph and Mary to the banqueting house. When the angel announced to Mary that she should be the mother of the Savior, she realized that she who was in the line of David would be the one who would bear this child. Notice what she says in her Magnificat: "He hath filled the hungry with good things . . ." (Luke 1:53), using exactly the same picture as we have in the Song of Solomon: "He brought me to the banqueting house." What a picture we have here!

You recall in chapter 1, verse 4, the girl's prayer was, "Draw me, we will run after thee." We cannot know the ecstasy of this experience unless the Spirit of God gives us discernment and opens our eyes to behold Christ in His beauty and glory. Oh, my friend, let's not be satisfied with eating scraps or, like the prodigal son, getting down to eat with the pigs when God has prepared such a banquet for us!

## THE BANNER OF LOVE

"He brought me to the banqueting house, and his banner over me was love." That banner is still floating over us today. The banner in that day had many meanings. Armies would carry banners with them when they went to war. I think all the various meanings of banners are included when she says, "His banner over me was love."

The banner of an army, as, for example, the banners of the Roman legions, was an emblem of conquest. The Son of God still goes forth to war. There is a battle today for the souls of men. I remember how I resisted Him. I shall never forget the excuses I made for not going to a young people's conference. I thought they were a bunch of sissies who were going there, and I didn't want to go with that crowd. I wasn't interested. But, you know, He opened up the way, and the first thing I knew I was there. Before I knew it, I had made a decision in my heart for Him. His banner over me was a banner of conquest.

The banner is also an emblem of protection. When the Lord Jesus came into this world, the Father testified, ". . . This is my beloved Son, in whom I am well pleased" (Matt. 3:17), and the enemies of Jesus could not touch Him until His hour had come. He was protected. When the time had come, they took Him and crucified Him. We will never understand how terrible that was. He cried out in that hour, ". . . My God, my God, why hast thou forsaken me?" (Matt. 27:46). His enemies thought that since God had forsaken Him they could do as they pleased with Him. They mocked Him, saying, "He trusted in God; let him deliver him now, if he will have him: for he said, I am the Son of God" (Matt. 27:43). But God *was* still pleased with His Son; He delighted in Him, and He raised Him from the dead. He delivered Him from death. And now that banner of salvation and protection is over all those who are His. "And the peace of God, which passeth all understanding, shall keep [that is, be on guard duty over] your hearts and minds through Christ Jesus" (Phil 4:7). He will protect you.

The banner is also an emblem of enlistment. You can enlist as a soldier. By the way, His army is entirely a volunteer army. "I beseech you therefore, brethren, by the mercies of God, that ye present your bodies a living sacrifice, holy, acceptable unto God, which is your reasonable service" (Rom. 12:1). "If ye love me, keep my commandments" (John 14:15). What if you don't love Him? Then forget it! This is a banner for enlistment on a voluntary basis. "His banner over me was love."

## LOVESICK

**Stay me with flagons, comfort me with apples: for I am sick of love [Song 2:5].**

The Holy Spirit of God has brought the saved soul into a personal relationship with Christ that is satisfying. I repeat: God is satisfied with Jesus and what He did for you. Are you satisfied? Do you find joy and satisfaction and delight in the person of Christ? Spend time in this Song of Solomon. Great men of God down through the ages have spent time in this book, men like Moody and McCheyne. Personally, I have spent too little time in this book, but it has become very meaningful to me.

When I went to Nashville, Tennessee, to pastor a church, I succeeded a great man of God. I always loved to go out to visit him. I never talked to that man without learning something new from the Word of God. One day he told me, "Vernon, the other night I was lying in bed, and I thought how wonderful Christ is. It just seemed to me that there was glory all around my bed. Don't misunderstand—I was not seeing things. It was just so wonderful to contemplate the person of Christ. Finally my body was so worked up that I couldn't go to sleep, and I had to cry out to God, 'Oh Lord, turn off the glory. This old body of mine can't stand any more of it.'" Imagine the experience of Paul when he was caught up to the third heaven! You see, most of us haven't even gotten our foot in the door yet. We know so little about what it is to have this kind of fellowship with Him. Of course it will have its final fulfillment when we come to "the marriage supper of the Lamb."

Erskine, who has written many wonderful things, expressed it like this:

The love, the love that I bespeak,
Works wonders in the soul;
For when I'm whole it makes me sick,
When sick, it makes me whole.

I'm overcome, I faint, I fail,
Till love shall love relieve;
More love divine the wound can heal,
Which love divine did give.

More of the joy that makes me faint,
Would give me present ease;
If more should kill me, I'm content
To die of that disease.

This wonderful love of God is a paradox. We long for it, and yet the glory of it all is more than we can bear.

**His left hand is under my head, and his right hand doth embrace me [Song 2:6].**

"His left hand is under my head"—He is able to save us to the uttermost. "His right hand doth embrace me"—He is able to keep us from temptation and protect you and me down here.

**I charge you, O ye daughters of Jerusalem, by the roes, and by the hinds of the field, that ye stir not up, nor awake my love, till he please [Song 2:7].**

What is it that will wake Him up? What is it that would disturb Him in His fellowship with you? It is the sin and waywardness in your life. Not only are we to be satisfied with Him, but, oh, that He might be satisfied with us!

We have come now to the second song. Apparently, Solomon has been away on a trip. The bride has been looking forward in great anticipation to his coming home. What a wonderful thing it is to see the excitement of the bride as she looks forward to the coming of the bridegroom. We will find its final fulfillment, I believe, in the anticipation of the church for the return of Christ to take the church out of the world.

## THE VOICE OF THE BELOVED

**The voice of my beloved! behold, he cometh leaping upon the mountains, skipping upon the hills [Song 2:8].**

"The voice of my beloved!" The Lord Jesus had this to say concerning His voice: "My sheep hear my voice, and I know them, and they follow me: And I give unto them eternal life; and they shall never perish, neither shall any man pluck them out of my hand" (John 10:27–28). "The voice of my beloved! behold, he cometh. . . ." Have you ever considered that at the Rapture of the church it is the voice of the Son of God that is to be heard? The church is made up of those people who have heard about Him. We have heard of His death and burial and resurrection. We have trusted Him. We listen to Him today, so when He comes we are going to know His voice. Jesus said, "My sheep hear My voice." The sheep know who He is.

When the Lord Jesus comes to take His church out of this world, ". . . the Lord himself [He will come personally] shall descend from heaven with a shout, with the voice of the archangel, and with the trump of God . . ." (1 Thess. 4:16). The "shout," the "voice," and the "trump" are all *His* voice. "The voice of my beloved! behold, he cometh." What a picture of the Rapture!

Contrast this to the coming of the Lord Jesus to rule and to reign on this earth. Then it will not be the sound of a voice but a tremendous sight of glory. The appeal is not to the ear as it is in the Rapture; the appeal is to the eye when He comes to the earth. "And then shall appear the sign of the Son of man in heaven: and then shall all the tribes of the earth mourn, and they shall see the Son of man coming in the clouds of heaven with power and great glory" (Matt. 24:30). But at the Rapture it will be the "voice of my beloved!"

"Behold, he cometh leaping upon the mountains, skipping upon the hills." This is poetic language, of course. This is a song, and God is trying to speak to us through it.

There is a great deal said about the feet of Jesus. In fact, I developed a series of messages several years ago about the members of the body of the Lord Jesus Christ. I spoke of the eyes of Jesus that were stained with tears. I spoke of the lips of Jesus, and I spoke of His hands. I spoke of the feet of Jesus.

"He maketh my feet like hinds' feet, and setteth me upon my high places" (Ps. 18:33). *Aijeleth Shahar,* which means the "hind of the morning," is the title to Psalm 22. It reveals the Lord Jesus Christ in the day of His sorrow, in His suffering and death upon the cross. It is a picture of the hind of the morning. All night long the dogs had been following the hind. They had torn at his flesh. They had attempted to destroy him. "For dogs have compassed me: the assembly of the wicked have enclosed me: they pierced my hands and my feet"(Ps. 22:16). But when the sun comes up, what do we find? He is the hind of the morning, standing on the mountain peak. He has been delivered out of death. He is coming back, my friend. He is skipping upon the hills; He is leaping upon the mountains. I can't think of a more wonderful, more poetic picture of the Lord Jesus Christ in His return to earth.

I like the way Erskine expresses it:

> When manifold obstructions met,
> My willing Saviour made
> A stepping-stone of every let,
> That in his way was laid.

He took stumbling blocks and made them into stepping stones. He made a way for us, and He *is* the way for us. We have the picture of Him coming again, this One who is the hind, or the roe, or the young hart who is leaping upon the mountains and skipping upon the hills.

Now He is drawing closer—

> The voice of my Beloved sounds,
> Over the rocks and rising grounds;

O'er hills of guilt, and seas of grief,
He leaps, he flies to my relief.

## BEHIND OUR WALL

**My beloved is like a roe or a young hart: behold, he standeth behind our wall, he looketh forth at the windows, shewing himself through the lattice [Song 2:9].**

Today He stands behind the wall. He has gone to be at God's right hand, and we are way down here. It is like the time He went to the mountain to pray after He had fed the five thousand, and His disciples were down on the Sea of Galilee in a storm. That is the way it is today. I am down here in a storm; He is up yonder at God's right hand.

He is on the other side of the wall, and everything under the sun is trying to keep us from Him: the world, the flesh, and the devil. But He still says to us the same thing that He said to Zacchaeus: ". . . Make haste, and come down; for today I must abide at thy house" (Luke 19:5). He still tells us that he wants to come in and sup with us, as He went into the home of that old publican and had fellowship with him. He will come to you if you will invite Him in. This is the One of whom John the Baptist said, ". . . there standeth one among you, whom ye know not" (John 1:26). And today the world does not know Him. He is behind a wall—a wall of indifference, a wall of rebellion against God, a wall of sin. What a picture!

## THE SONG OF HIS RETURN

**My beloved spake, and said unto me, Rise up, my love, my fair one, and come away.**

**For, lo, the winter is past, the rain is over and gone;**

**The flowers appear on the earth; the time of the singing of birds is come, and the voice of the turtle is heard in our land;**

**The fig tree putteth forth her green figs, and the vines with the tender grape give a good smell. Arise, my love, my fair one, and come away [Song 2:10-13].**

"Rise up, my love, my fair one, and come away." Christ loved the church and gave Himself for it. He did it because He is going to come to take the church out of this world. He is going to present it to Himself as a church that is purified—all of us believers need that purifying. He sanctifies and cleanses us with the washing of water by the Word. That is the reason we have Bible study. He wants to present to Himself a glorious church, without a spot or wrinkle. He wants it to be holy and without blemish. That is why He calls, "Arise, my love, my fair one, and come away."

"For, lo, the winter is past"—it is cold down here in this world.

"The rain is over and gone"—the storms of life will then have abated. Are you having a hard time today, Christian friend? Christ said you would: ". . . In the world ye shall have tribulation . . ." (John 16:33). Don't be upset if you are having trouble. It is one of the marks that you belong to Him, that you are a child of God. But when He comes, all the trouble will be over. He will wipe away all tears from your eyes. Every broken heart will be healed. Every sorrow will have vanished away when we are in His presence. "The winter is past, the rain is over and gone."

"The flowers appear on the earth." When the Lord Jesus comes for His own and takes them out of this world to the beautiful home which He has prepared, I believe it will be to a beautiful garden of flowers. I like to think that in the New Jerusalem there will be a profusion of flowers.

"The time of the singing of birds is come, and the voice of the turtle [turtledove] is heard in our land." "The time of the singing of birds" is another very lovely expression. There is going to be a great deal of singing when we come into His presence.

Have you ever noticed that there is a great deal of singing that opens the story of the Gospels? Dr. Luke is the writer who starts farther back in the account of the birth of Christ than any of the other Gospel writers, and he recorded the songs. There is the song of Zacharias, the song of Elisabeth, the song of Mary, the song of Anna, and the song of Simeon. There were a lot of songs connected with His birth. The church began singing, and the joy of these people is what called attention to them in the Roman world. Some day when we come into His presence we will sing a new song to the Lord, for He has done wondrous things! I can't sing it now because God didn't create me with a voice that could sing, but when I have a new body, I'm going to sing that new song. Until then I can lift my heart in the praise that is due Him. The very singing of the birds of the air and the bursting buds of the flowers of the earth should remind us of the debt of joyful gratitude we owe for His great salvation. Kingwellmersh expressed it poetically:

> O sing unto this glittering glorious king,
> O praise his name let every living thing;
> Let heart and voice, like belles of silver, ring
> The comfort that this day did bring.

It is interesting to note that in our older Bibles "the time of singing" is rendered "the time of pruning." The season of the singing of birds is also the season of the pruning of the vines. The branch that is pruned for fruit and the song that is pruned for beauty are expressed in the same way by the Hebrew writers, which makes it difficult to determine whether "singing" or "pruning" is intended. Pruning the vines is exactly what the Lord Jesus said He was going to do. He said, "I am the true [genuine] vine, and my Father is the husbandman. Every branch in me that beareth not fruit he taketh away: and every branch that beareth fruit, he purgeth [or prunes] it, that it may bring forth more fruit" (John 15:1–2). My friend, you and I are living in the time of pruning, but the time of singing is ahead of us. What a picture this is!

"The voice of the turtle [turtledove] is heard in our land." The turtledove is the wild dove which is common today. I saw them in Israel. They looked very similar to the doves in California, only I think they were somewhat smaller. The dove has always been the emblem of peace. The reason for that is that the dove went out and brought back an olive leaf to Noah after the waters of the Flood had receded. That spoke of peace, because the judgment was over.

Also the turtledove speaks to us of our salvation which is complete because the judgment is past. It is past because Christ bore the judgment for us. He has endured it in our behalf. I am saved, not because of who I am, but because of what *Christ* did. My friend, your sins are either on you or they are on Christ. If your sins are on you, you are yet to come up for judgment. If you have trusted Christ, your sins are on Him. He bore them for you, and the judgment is past. By faith you appropriate the salvation. The turtledove speaks of the peace that He has made for us.

This is the reason that not just a *few* of the saints will go to meet Christ at the Rapture. There are some folk who believe that only the super-duper saints will go. However, the hope of *every* believer is to be taken with Christ when He comes for His church. We will go to be with Him, not because we have been super-duper saints, but because He has made peace by the blood of His cross. The turtledove is symbolic of this.

The "turtle" is the turtledove of the morning. Where I live, the turtledove is the first bird to get up in the morning. It heralds a new day that is coming. I love the way Isaac Watts has expressed it—evidently he spent a great deal of time studying the Song of Solomon:

> The legal wintery state is gone,
> The mists are fled, the spring comes on;
> The sacred turtle-dove we hear
> Proclaim the new, the joyful year.
> And when we hear Christ Jesus say,
> Rise up my Love, and come away,
> Our hearts would fain outfly the wind,
> And leave all earthly joys behind.

"The fig tree putteth forth her green figs, and the vines with the tender grape give a good smell"—these are signs of springtime. "Arise, my love, my fair one, and come away." First Thessalonians 4:16 tells us that ". . . the dead in Christ shall rise first." The Lord Jesus said, ". . . I go to prepare a place for you. And if I go and prepare a place for you, I will come again, and receive you unto myself; that where I am, there ye may be also" (John 14:2-3). "Rise up, my love, my fair one, and come away."

## THE DOVE IN THE CLEFTS OF THE ROCK

**O my dove, that art in the clefts of the rock, in the secret places of the stairs, let me see thy countenance, let me hear thy voice; for sweet is thy voice, and thy countenance is comely [Song 2:14].**

The psalmist made this plea: "O deliver not the soul of thy turtledove unto the multitude of the wicked . . ." (Ps. 74:19). Will the Lord deliver us? We are told He will hide us in the clefts of the rock, and that Rock symbolizes Christ. He is the Rock upon whom the church is built. He bore our judgment, and we can rest in Him. That should bring us not only satisfaction but also security. If you are on the Rock today, you are safe. Even if you do not recognize the assurance of this, you are still safe. A little Scottish lady was speaking with great assurance about her salvation. Someone said, "You act as if you were safe and secure on the Rock." She answered, "I am. Sometimes I do tremble on the Rock, but the Rock never trembles under me."

The dove is also an emblem for the Holy Spirit. He descended like a dove on the Lord Jesus. And everyone who is in Christ has that dove-like Spirit dwelling in him. ". . . if any man have not the Spirit of Christ, he is none of his" (Rom. 8:9). And true believers are like doves in their simplicity and their gentleness. Our Lord admonished us to be ". . . wise as serpents, and harmless as doves" (Matt. 10:16). Now, I suspect that a dove is a rather stupid bird. The other day as I was driving along, I accidentally hit a dove. The crazy dove stood there on the highway without making a move until the car was about to hit him. I regretted doing that, but I said, "You stupid little bird for staying there like you did!" You see, you and I need not only to be as harmless as doves, but we had better be as wise as serpents in our world today—or we'll get run over also.

The dove is a timid bird. The Lord says, "They shall tremble as a bird out of Egypt, and as a dove out of the land of Assyria: and I will place them in their houses, saith the LORD" (Hos. 11:11). The dove needs a hiding place in the clefts of the rock. Christ is a beautiful picture of the Rock who was wounded for us. As someone has said, "I got into the heart of Christ through a spear wound." Augustus M. Toplady's wonderful hymn is based on this thought.

> Rock of Ages, cleft for me,
> Let me hide myself in Thee;
> Let the water and the blood,
> From Thy wounded side which flowed,
> Be of sin the double cure,
> Cleanse me from its guilt and power. . . .
>
> Nothing in my hand I bring,
> Simply to Thy cross I cling;
> Naked, come to Thee for dress,
> Helpless, look to Thee for grace;
> Foul, I to the fountain fly;
> Wash me, Saviour, or I die.
>
> While I draw this fleeting breath,
> When my eyelids close in death,
> When I soar to worlds unknown,
> See Thee on Thy judgment throne,
> Rock of Ages, cleft for me,
> Let me hide myself in Thee.

## THE LITTLE FOXES

**Take us the foxes, the little foxes, that spoil the vines: for our vines have tender grapes [Song 2:15].**

They could put up a fence or a wall that would keep out the big foxes, but they had trouble with the little foxes. Those little fellows could sneak through. They were the ones that would sneak in and destroy the grapes and tear up the young vines. This has a message for us. "Foxes" are both subtle sins and fox-like men who corrupt others. Both were resolutely dragged into the light of day by John the Baptist. Regarding the subtle sins, he said, ". . . He that hath two coats, let him impart to him that hath none; and he that hath meat, let him do likewise. . . . Exact no more than that which is appointed you. . . . Do violence to no man, neither accuse any falsely; and be content with your wages" (Luke 3:11, 13–14). Then John the Baptist pointed his finger at Herod whom our Lord called "that old fox" (see Luke 13:32) and told him that he had no right to be married to another man's wife. I tell you, a preacher doesn't make himself popular when he says that kind of thing! Old Herod had John the Baptist killed by chopping off his head.

However, it is the young foxes that get into the contemporary church and cause trouble. The little sins spoil the fellowship among believers and spoil a Christian's life. For example there are the little sins of omission. "Therefore to him that knoweth to do good, and doeth it not, to him it is sin" (James 4:17). Here is one of those little foxes. This is the sin of omission. How often do we see something that we should do for God, but we didn't do it? How often have we sinned in this way? We are told that the Lord Jesus went about doing good.

> I read
> In a book
> Where a man called
> Christ
> Went about doing good.
> It is very disconcerting
> To me
> That I am so easily
> Satisfied
> With just
> Going about.
> —Author unknown

How often we have intended to write a letter, but we didn't write it. How often we have intended to do something for missions, but we neglected to do it. How many times we should have been praying for someone, but we neglected to pray. We think of the words of the prophet Samuel: ". . . God forbid that I should sin against the LORD in ceasing to pray for you . . ." (1 Sam. 12:23). These are little sins of omission. They are the little foxes that spoil the vineyard.

Here is another of those little foxes: ". . . whatsoever is not of faith is sin" (Rom. 14:23). How often do we take a step on our own, but we try to call it a step of faith. We know it is not really faith; we know we just want to have our way. That is a sin. It is a little fox. It gets in and spoils the work of God. We have a tendency to lean on that very lame and broken reed and try to hold ourselves up with it and maintain a pious attitude. We say, "I am doing this because God is leading me," when we know it is not true. We say it so lightly. Romans tells us that whatever we do that is not of faith is sin.

Showing partiality is another little fox that is seen among God's people. James lowers the boom on that: "But if ye have respect [show partiality] to persons, ye commit sin, and are convinced of the law as transgressors" (James 2:9). I have had this happen to me just as James described it. I went to a certain church just to visit, not wanting to be recognized. I wanted to hear the preacher. When I went in, the usher was absolutely insulting to me. He said, "You wait right here." Then he came back and said, "Well, I don't have a seat for you. You'll have to stand here in the back." He looked at me for a moment, then said, "Oh, you're Dr. McGee! I'll get a chair and let you sit right here!" How tragic it is to see in some churches a well-known or a wealthy man acknowledged in the service and some poor man, who probably is more godly, absolutely ignored. That is a little fox that really wrecks God's work in our day.

Then there is the little fox of not giving freely to God. It is not the amount of the giving that is the only thing that is wrong about it. It is the attitude of giving, the hypocrisy of it all. We sing songs such as, "Were the whole realm of nature mine, that were a present far too small"—then we put a quarter into the collection plate! We actually sing lies. We pretend we have given ourselves and all that we have to the Lord. Oh, my friend, it is the little foxes that are destroying a lot of the grapes today.

## THE NIGHT BEFORE DAYBREAK

The next wonderful statement follows closely after the song of the bridegroom's return, which is symbolic of the Rapture, that is, Christ's coming again for the church.

**My beloved is mine, and I am his: he feedeth among the lilies [Song 2:16].**

This Song of Solomon expresses the highest spiritual state of the relationship between the Lord Jesus Christ and the believer. There is no other book of the Bible which portrays this relationship any better than this little book, and there is no higher plane than this right here: "My beloved is mine, and I am his." This is one of the deepest, most profound of all theological truths which our Lord Jesus put into seven simple words: ". . . ye in me, and I in you" (John 14:20). The bride says, "My beloved is mine, and I am his."

The Lord Jesus said in effect, "Down here I took your place when I died on the cross. I am in you. Now you are to show forth My life down here in this world." (Of course we can only do that in the power of the Holy Spirit.) But we are in Him up there—seated in the heavenly places, accepted in the Beloved, joined to Him, risen with Christ. "If ye then be risen with Christ, seek those things which are above, where Christ sitteth on the right hand of God" (Col 3:1). How wonderful! Oh, my friend, if you are a child of God, why don't you tell Him that you love Him?

You and I live in a day when we may not have very much of this world's goods; yet we are rich. We don't glory men; we glory in Christ. "Therefore let no man glory in men. For all things are yours; Whether Paul, or Apollos, or Cephas, or the world, or life, or death, or things present, or things to come; all are yours; And ye are Christ's; and Christ is God's" (1 Cor. 3:21–23). We belong to Christ. He is ours. He belongs to us. He is our Savior. He is our Shepherd. We ought to draw very close to Him and appropriate these wonderful spiritual blessings that are ours. It is a high level of spiritual life when you and I can say, "My beloved is mine, and I am his."

"He feedeth among the lilies." This again refers to the flower-strewn couch upon which He reclines at the banqueting table. It speaks of satisfaction, of fellowship, of joy, of everything that is wonderful. This world is seeking these things. This world is looking for a good time. This world wants to "live it up." Well, let's have a good time and live it up by sitting at Christ's table and rejoicing in Him. This is a high spiritual level. I'm afraid that many of us do not ". . . attain unto it" (Ps. 139:6). Therefore we have to cry out as the bride did, "Draw me, we will run after thee." We can't run, we cannot run the race that is set before us until we not only see Jesus but *appropriate* His power in our lives. "My beloved is mine, and I am his."

**Until the day break, and the shadows flee away, turn, my beloved, and be thou like a roe or a young hart upon the mountains of Bether [Song 2:17].**

We come back to that picture of Christ as the hind of the morning. Remember that we saw Him on that bright morning (v. 8) standing on the mountain peak in triumph. All during the night the hunters had been after His life, and the fierce dogs had been leaping at Him. How terrible it was! He went down through the doorway of death, but He came up through the doorway of resurrection. Now, in light of that, although you and I are presently living in a dark world, we can look forward to the daybreak. My friend, let the redemption that you have in Christ and all that He has done for you be meaningful to you. Rest upon that. Let that be your comfort; let that be the pillow for your head during the dark hours of this life—"until the day break, and the shadows flee away."

# CHAPTER 3

As we begin chapter 3 we are still in the second song, but I would say that we have come to the second stanza of it. However, this does begin a new section, which is set in an altogether different scene.

At the beginning of this book we were up in the hill country of Ephraim where we saw a girl and her family who were tenant farmers. Now Solomon has won her heart and has brought her back with him to Jerusalem.

## THE MIDNIGHT SEARCH

**By night on my bed I sought him whom my soul loveth: I sought him, but I found him not.**

**I will rise now, and go about the city in the streets, and in the broad ways I will seek him whom my soul loveth: I sought him, but I found him not [Song 3:1–2].**

Now the scene has shifted to the palace in Jerusalem to which the king has taken her. She has been left alone—the king, perhaps, being away on business. What is recorded here is a dream that reflects the anguish of their separation in which she finally goes out to look for him in the streets of the city.

"By night on my bed I sought him." This has a marvelous spiritual application to our relationship with Christ. When we have a big day ahead of us, we think we must have a good night's sleep. If sleep is preferred to Christ, we may get in our eight hours, but we have lost Him who is far better than rest. A. Moody Stuart has put it like this: "But if Christ is first and best and most necessary, if he is more to us than food or sleep, he is often, though not always, quickly found, without actual loss either of the time or of the sleep which we were willing to sacrifice for his sake. Our sleep is then sweet unto us and refreshing, for the Lord himself is dwelling in us, and resting with us."

"I will rise now, and go about the city in the streets." The getting out of bed and going about the city in her search indicates a determination to seek the Lord.

"I sought him, but I found him not." This is her honest confession. A great many folk never find Christ because they never seek Him. Oh, how many Christians sit in a church pew every Sunday and never face honestly the fact: "I found Him not." However, He has promised that He will be found of those who seek Him with their whole heart. Or, as James put it, "Draw nigh to God, and he will draw nigh to you . . ." (James 4:8).

> **The watchmen that go about the city found me: to whom I said, Saw ye him whom my soul loveth? [Song 3:3].**

The watchmen seem to have been helpful in directing her to the Beloved. At least, it was only a short distance from them that she found Him.

> **It was but a little that I passed from them, but I found him whom my soul loveth: I held him, and would not let him go, until I had brought him into my mother's house, and into the chamber of her that conceived me [Song 3:4].**

Oh, my friend, what a tremendous reward for her search—"I found him whom my soul loveth!" Again I quote A. Moody Stuart (p. 231): "I found him—I, a man, found the Lord of Glory; I, a slave to sin, found the great Deliverer; I, the child of darkness, found the Light of life; I, the uttermost of the lost, found my Savior, and my God; I, widowed and desolate, found my Friend, my Beloved, my Husband! Go and do likewise, sons and daughters of Zion, and He will be found of you, 'for then shall ye find, when ye search with all your heart.'"

"I held him, and would not let him go." Maintaining unbroken fellowship with Christ requires effort on our part. It is easy to let other interests crowd into our lives so that we lose the sense of His presence. Stuart has well said, "Unheld, the King will go away; He is willing to be held, yet not willing to remain without being held." (This, of course, has no reference to a believer losing his salvation, but of losing his fellowship with Christ.)

"I . . . brought him into my mother's house, and into the chamber of her that conceived me." When she found Him, she went right back to the place where she had been born, where she had met Him. Many of us need to get back to that first love. Do you remember when you came to Christ? Do you remember how much He meant to you then?

> I charge you, O ye daughters of Jerusalem, by the roes, and by the hinds of the field, that ye stir not up, nor awake my love, till he please [Song 3:5].

Now that wonderful fellowship with Him is restored.

## THE ENTRANCE OF SOLOMON WITH HIS BRIDE

This last part of the chapter is a little gem in itself. It depicts the return of the king for his bride. This little Shulamite girl had waited a long time for the return of the shepherd to whom she had given her heart. One day she is out in the vineyard working. Down the road there comes a pillar of smoke, and the cry is passed along from one group of peasants to another, "Behold, King Solomon is coming!"—but she has work to do. Then someone comes to her excitedly, saying, "Oh, king Solomon is asking for you!" Mystified, she says, "Asking for me? I don't know king Solomon!" But when she is brought into his presence, she recognizes that he is her shepherd-lover who has come for her.

He places her at his side in the royal chariot and the procession sweeps on, leaving the amazed country folk speechless at the sudden change in the position of her who had been just one of them.

How beautifully this pictures the glorious reality of the return of Christ, our Beloved, when He comes for His own. "For the Lord himself shall descend from heaven with a shout, with the voice of the archangel, and with the trump of God: and the dead in Christ shall rise first: Then we which are alive and remain shall be caught up together with them in the clouds to meet the Lord in the air: and so shall we ever be with the Lord" (1 Thess. 4:16–17).

**Who is this that cometh out of the wilderness like pillars of smoke, perfumed with myrrh and frankincense, with all powders of the merchant? [Song 3:6].**

This is a description of Solomon as he rides into Jerusalem with his bride. The glory that was Solomon's is beyond description. We will get a glimpse of it in the next few verses.

We as believers are to go through this world as witnesses of the Lord Jesus Christ. As witnesses we are made new in Christ. Each of us is like the bride who is brought before the Bridegroom and the fragrance of Christ should be upon us as we witness to the world— "perfumed with myrrh and frankincense." How wonderful the Lord Jesus is! The myrrh speaks of His death and the frankincense of His life. Both were sweet; both were glorious.

**Behold his bed, which is Solomon's; threescore valiant men are about it, of the valiant of Israel [Song 3:7].**

His "bed" is the traveling couch in which the King is carried by bearers.

"Threescore valiant men are about it, of the valiant of Israel." They are living in days of danger. These are the guards, and they are there for his protection. They are the Secret Service men who have charge of his person to watch over him.

May I say that I think that we need to guard the person of the Lord Jesus. In other words we need to declare our belief in the deity of Jesus Christ, that He was God manifest in the flesh. We must reject the teaching of liberalism. We must reject anything that makes Him just a human Jesus. He was God manifest in the flesh.

**They all hold swords, being expert in war: every man hath his sword upon his thigh because of fear in the night [Song 3:8].**

Notice that the guards all have swords. The Scriptures tell us that our sword is the Word of God. They are "expert in war." And we need to know how to use the Word of God. The Word of God is the sword of the Spirit, and that is the weapon of a good soldier of Jesus Christ.

**King Solomon made himself a chariot of the wood of Lebanon.**

**He made the pillars thereof of silver, the bottom thereof of gold, the covering of it of purple, the midst thereof being paved with love, for the daughters of Jerusalem [Song 3:9–10].**

He has a chariot made out of the cedars of Lebanon. "The bottom thereof of gold"—imagine, the floor made of gold!
"The midst thereof being paved with love, for [or from] the daughters of Jerusalem." Solomon's chariot is adorned by the needlework of the women of Jerusalem. What beauty there is. But, also, what tremendous emotion and love is displayed there.

**Go forth, O ye daughters of Zion, and behold king Solomon with the crown wherewith his mother crowned him in the day of his espousals, and in the day of the gladness of his heart [Song 3:11].**

It says, "his mother crowned him." If you go back to the story in 1 Kings 1, you will find that David didn't really want to crown him. Another son of David, Adonijah, was carrying on a bit of strategy and was trying to get to the throne himself. David was an old man, and he didn't do anything at all about the situation. His favorite son, Absalom, had been killed, and David just didn't seem to have much heart for Solomon. So Nathan the prophet went to Bathsheba, the mother of

Solomon, and said, "We'd better get busy or Adonijah may become the new king." So Bathsheba and Nathan went to king David, and king David said, "Well, bring him in. We'll make him the king." That is the way Solomon was made the king of Israel. I like the way it is stated here: "his *mother* crowned him." It was his mother who was interested in him. I really think that David was not much interested in making Solomon the new king, even though he was David's son.

"Behold king Solomon." This is a picture of Christ. Behold Him. Behold Him in His birth. Behold Him in His life. Behold Him in His death. Behold Him in His resurrection. Behold Him in His glory today. And behold Him as the One who is coming again for His bride.

# CHAPTER 4

This entire chapter except the last verse is the song of the bridegroom. It expresses Solomon's love for this girl whom he had met up in the hill country and had brought to town, as it were. I suppose that she wore shoes for the first time. Now she is wearing lovely dresses, and she sits at the table of Solomon. What a privilege she had, and she was rejoicing in it.

As we read this chapter, we should see that the Spirit of God is trying to show us Christ's love for us. It is expressed through this very wonderful and personal relationship. It shows to us the love of Christ for the church and His love for the individual believer. This is the love song of the Bridegroom, or the love song of the Lord Jesus Christ.

It is obvious that He speaks of the church when He says, "Thou art all fair, my love; there is no spot in thee" (v. 7). This is Christ speaking of the church, of the believer; He is speaking to you and me. Does that mean then that we are going to have to become perfect? Oh, no. In Ephesians Paul says, ". . . as Christ also loved the church, and gave himself for it; That he might sanctify and cleanse it with the washing of water by the word" (Eph. 5:25–26). He's already cleansed us by the blood; through His sacrifice we have the forgiveness of sin, so that there is no charge brought against us. But He is also going to sanctify us and cleanse us by the Word of God. "That he might present it to himself a glorious church, not having spot, or wrinkle, or any such thing; but that it should be holy and without blemish" (Eph. 5:27). He will be the One who will make the church without spot or wrinkle—we will be seen in Christ. Now He can look at the church and say, "Thou art all fair, my love; there is no spot in thee" because He removed the spot from the church and from each believer.

**Behold, thou art fair, my love; behold thou art fair; thou hast doves' eyes within thy locks: thy hair is as a flock of goats, that appear from mount Gilead [Song 4:1].**

We find here a very minute description of this girl. It describes the parts of her body, if you please. Now there are two extreme viewpoints of marriage. One is that the emphasis is put upon sex. The other is that there is no emphasis put on sex, that marriage is such a high, holy state that sex doesn't enter into it at all. But when the emphasis is placed completely on sex, then the relationship becomes more like that between two animals. True marriage lies between these two extreme viewpoints. When the bridegroom holds the bride in his arms, their love, their physical love, is consummated.

**Thy teeth are like a flock of sheep that are even shorn, which came up from the washing; whereof every one bear twins, and none is barren among them.**

**Thy lips are like a thread of scarlet, and thy speech is comely: thy temples are like a piece of a pomegranate within thy locks [Song 4:2-3].**

This is how the bridegroom sees the bride. I'm sure every young fellow has looked into the eyes of some girl and told her what beautiful eyes she has. I met my wife when she was a young schoolteacher. She had black hair, black as a raven's wing, and dark brown eyes. Today there is some gray hair. I tell you, when I met her, I thought her hair was beautiful, and I told her so. I told her she had beautiful eyes. Now I never told her she had beautiful big toes because I really don't think her big toes are beautiful. But I do think she is beautiful.

This reveals to us that the Lord Jesus not only loves us but the Lord Jesus knows us. We need to quit kidding ourselves because we are not kidding Him at all. This means that we can go to Him and tell Him everything. There is no use in trying to cover up, no use in trying to use subterfuge, no use in trying to beat around the bush. We can tell

Him everything that we have on our hearts. We can tell Him all about our weaknesses, about our sin, about all the things that are in our hearts and lives. That is the way to deal with them.

Do you have an inferiority complex? Then tell the Lord Jesus about it. He is the only One who has an answer for that. An eminent Christian psychologist here in Southern California years ago told me, "You can't get rid of an inferiority complex. All that the psychologist can do is shift an inferiority complex from one place in the personality to another. The only place where anyone finds a solution to it is at the Cross of Christ." I believe that is where people should go with their complexes. Augustine said that our hearts are restless until we come to the Lord. Paul wrote, "I can do all things through Christ which strengtheneth me" (Phil. 4:13). Maybe you don't even need to get rid of your inferiority complex. It may help you to find your strength in Him. It may keep you from being a proud, arrogant Christian. It may help you give all the glory to Him.

Do you have a bad habit which you would like to change? Then go to Him and confess it. He is rich in mercy. I think that for years I must have gone to Him two or three hundred times to tell Him about something. He was rich in mercy to me, which means He has a whole lot of it. Although I failed again and again, I kept going back in repentance. It was wonderful to go to Him. Do you know what happened? When the time came, He gave me the victory in *His* way. Our Lord moves in a mysterious way His wonders to perform. He doesn't follow my rules or your rules. He doesn't do it through some gimmick which men have worked out. He helps in His own time and His own way.

May I say to you, He knows us intimately. He knows every tiny detail of our lives. We should never be afraid to go to Him and tell Him everything.

> **Until the day break, and the shadows flee away, I will get me to the mountain of myrrh, and to the hill of frankincense [Song 4:6].**

This is the place where we need to go for the solution to our problems. "The mountain of myrrh" is symbolic of the Cross of Christ because myrrh speaks of His death. That is where you will find comfort and salvation and help and hope.

"The hill of frankincense" refers to His life, but not simply His earthly life. Paul writes, "Wherefore henceforth know we no man after the flesh: yea, though we have known Christ after the flesh, yet now henceforth know we him no more" (2 Cor. 5:16)—now we know Him as the glorified Christ.

The solution to your problem is in knowing Christ. "Let this mind be in you, which was also in Christ Jesus" (Phil. 2:5). That, my friend, is the reason that I keep saying the answer is in the Word of God. It is ignorance of His Word that causes people to search elsewhere for answers. It makes a person vulnerable to false teachers who trade on and take advantage of those who are ignorant of the Word of God. But it is through the Word of God that we get acquainted with Jesus Christ and learn to sit at that round table in the banqueting hall which we have seen here in the Song of Solomon. There we can feast with Him, and find satisfaction and joy in Him.

You and I do not realize how much He really loves us. Listen to Him:

> **Thou hast ravished my heart, my sister, my spouse; thou hast ravished my heart with one of thine eyes, with one chain of thy neck.**

> **How fair is thy love, my sister, my spouse! how much better is thy love than wine! and the smell of thine ointments than all spices! [Song 4:9–10].**

The bridegroom speaking of the bride typifies the Lord Jesus speaking of believers, those who are His own. This is how much He loves us today. Oh, it would break your heart and my heart if we knew how much He loves us. Only the Spirit of God can make this love real to us. Some folks write out a little motto and stick it on their car bumper and then drive around with it. It says, "Jesus loves you." I wonder, how do you know He loves you? Have you experienced that love yourself? Are you conscious of His love right now? Oh, my friend, He loves you! Fall in love with Him.

Now the bride speaks:

**Awake, O north wind; and come, thou south; blow upon my garden, that the spices thereof may flow out. Let my beloved come into his garden, and eat his pleasant fruits [Song 4:16].**

Remember how the Lord Jesus taught His disciples in the Upper Room in that wonderful discourse that is found in John 13—17. In the midst of it, in John 14, we find that the Lord Jesus is interpreted again and again by the disciples asking Him questions. The last one to interrupt Him was Judas. Have you ever noticed the question which he asked the Lord? "Judas saith unto him, not Iscariot, Lord, how is it that thou wilt manifest thyself unto us, and not unto the world?" (John 14:22). He is saying in effect, "Lord, it is wonderful to be here. You are revealing these wonderful truths about Yourself to us, but what about the world outside?"

Now the bride is getting the message. "O north wind"—that north wind is cold, and it may cause the bride to get very cold. But, "*Awake, O north wind.*" Why? That this spice, this wonderful fragrance might be blown out to others and they might enjoy it. Dr. Ironside adds: "It indicates her yearning desire to be all that he would have her to be." The north wind, he continues, is "that cold, bitter, biting, wintry blast. Naturally she would shrink from that as we all would, and yet the cold of winter is as necessary as the warmth of summer if there is going to be perfection in fruitbearing. It takes the cold to bring out the flavor of apples. And it is so with our lives. We need the north winds of adversity and trial as well as the zephyrs of the south so agreeable to our natures. The very things we shrink from are the experiences that will work in us to produce the peaceable fruits of righteousness. If everything were easy and soft and beautiful in our lives, they would be insipid; there would be so little in them for God that could delight His heart; and so there must be the north wind as well as the south."

It is this kind of life that the Lord Jesus uses to reach the world. He has not forgotten the world.

The bride says to her beloved, "Let my beloved come into his gar-

den, and eat his pleasant fruits." This is an invitation he will accept.
And in that Upper Room the Lord Jesus said to His questioning disciples, ". . . If a man love me, he will keep my words: and my Father will
love him, and we will come unto him, and make our abode with him"
(John 14:23).

# CHAPTER 5

In this chapter there seems to be a certain amount of conflict in the mind of the bride about whether they should spend time in fellowship and communion or in going out to discharge their responsibilities. Both are essential. We need to be doing both. We need to sit at the feet of Jesus, but we also need to follow those feet as they go out on the hillsides looking for the lost sheep. We need to follow those feet out into the world, which is a field in which to plant the seed of the Word of God.

> **I am come into my garden, my sister, my spouse: I have gathered my myrrh with my spice; I have eaten my honeycomb with my honey; I have drunk my wine with my milk: eat, O friends; drink, yea, drink abundantly, O beloved [Song 5:1].**

He is inviting her to join with him in fellowship. Our Lord says, "Behold, I stand at the door, and knock: if any man hear my voice, and open the door, I will come in to him, and will sup with him, and he with me" (Rev. 3:20). That is the fellowship we need. And in connection with fellowship, John writes, ". . . These things write we unto you, that your joy may be full" (1 John 1:4). Not only does He want us to have fellowship, but He wants us to have a good time. Are you having a good time as a Christian?

Wonderful letters come to me in response to our radio broadcasts. There are people in hospitals and in rest homes who tell about their sufferings and the diseases with which they are afflicted. But they also write about the wonderful fellowship they have with the Lord Jesus. The tears came to my eyes when I read a letter from one dear lady, who wrote, "At night when the nurse tucks me in I cannot sleep but lie awake for another hour or two. During that time I pray for you until I go to sleep. Then I wake up about 4:30 in the morning and I pray for you again." Then she continues in her letter to tell how wonderful it is to have fellowship with the Lord Jesus. That is beautiful!

## THE WAKING SLEEP

Now we come to the fourth canticle, or the fourth song. These are like folk songs.

Now it is the bride who speaks.

> **I sleep, but my heart waketh: it is the voice of my beloved that knocketh, saying, Open to me, my sister, my love, my dove, my undefiled: for my head is filled with dew, and my locks with the drops of the night [Song 5:2].**

She says her heart is awake. She is on the alert, watching for him.

"The voice of my beloved"—he has been busy out in the night while the bride crawled into bed.

The church needs to hear this message today. All believers need to hear this message. Let's get out of bed and get busy. If the Lord has given us health, let us start moving out for Him.

> **I have put off my coat; how shall I put it on? I have washed my feet; how shall I defile them? [Song 5:3].**

Now she starts to rationalize. She is already in bed. She has washed her feet to go to bed, and she doesn't want to get out of bed and get her feet dirty.

> **My beloved put in his hand by the hole of the door, and my bowels were moved for him [Song 5:4].**

Her "bowels," that is, her emotions, were moved for him.

**I rose up to open to my beloved; and my hands dropped
with myrrh, and my fingers with sweet smelling
myrrh, upon the handles of the lock [Song 5:5].**

The background for this was a lovely custom that they had in that day.
When a man was in love with a girl and wanted to express his love, he
would go to her home and instead of leaving a calling card, he would
leave a fragrance. The door was so constructed as to leave an opening
so that one could reach through to the inside and remove the bar unless it was locked as well as barred—which was the case on this occasion. When there was no response from the sleeping bride, the
bridegroom placed myrrh on the inside handle of the door to let her
know that he had been there. Then she finally came to open the door,
the wonderful fragrance was transferred to her fingers. He had left the
sweetness of his presence.

The bride is a picture of the church today. The church doesn't go
very far from home. Very few get out from under the shadow of the
church steeple. Most folk don't even get off the church steps. As a
result, they have lost fellowship with the Lord Jesus. Actually, that is
one of those little foxes which destroy the grapes. We lose our fellowship when we step out of the will of God. That is what it means to
quench the Spirit (see 1 Thess. 5:19). It is quenching the Spirit to
refuse to go where He wants us to go or to do what He wants us to do.

I think that if we today would get up off our beds, begin to move out
and start doing something for God, we would find the sweetness of His
presence on the handle of our own bed chamber. We would experience
the sweetness of His fellowship.

This is the briefest of the songs, but what a little gem it is!

## THE SORROWING SEARCH FOR THE BELOVED

Now we come to the fifth song. In this love story king Solomon has
brought this humble Shulamite girl from the hill country of Ephraim
to the palace in Jerusalem. In these songs the bride reveals how impressed she is by everything there—the palace, the throne, and the

banquet table of the king. Her song includes her worship and adoration of the king.

But when he came to rouse her to come with him as he was out doing his work as a shepherd, looking for the sheep that were lost, she didn't want to get out of bed. When she finally did go to the door, he was gone. She opened the door and called to him, then she went out to look for him.

> **I opened to my beloved; but my beloved had withdrawn himself, and was gone: my soul failed when he spake: I sought him, but I could not find him; I called him, but he gave me no answer [Song 5:6].**

You see, the fellowship had been broken.

I personally believe that there are a great many Christians who have down one of two things: they have grieved the Spirit by sin in their lives, or they have quenched the Spirit by not being obedient to Him. That breaks fellowship with Him and causes us to lose our joy. It does not mean that we lose our salvation, but we will surely lose the *joy* of our salvation. It does not mean that we have lost the Holy Spirit. He still indwells the believer. We can grieve Him, but we cannot grieve Him away. However, we certainly can lose fellowship with Him, and many Christians are in that position.

Sometime ago a man said to me, "You speak of the reality of Christ in your life. I don't have it." That was a dead giveaway that he was quenching the Spirit of God. He was out of the will of God. I know the man quite well, and I believe the problem was that he was doing what *he* wanted to do instead of doing what he knew was the will of God. A person can try to mask the truth and say that he is doing the will of God. If he does not have the joy of the Lord, it is a giveaway that he is actually doing his own will.

The bride here has lost her fellowship. I tell you, if you are not doing something for the Lord, you haven't lost your salvation, but you surely are missing sweet fellowship with Him.

**The watchmen that went about the city found me, they
smote me, they wounded me; the keepers of the walls
took away my veil from me [Song 5:7].**

Do you realize how impotent and powerless we are if we attempt to go
out on our own? We may go out with a great deal of enthusiasm, but
enthusiasm will never replace fellowship with Him. Today there is a
lot of enthusiasm for knocking on doors and witnessing to people.
There are certain people who ought to be doing that; there are others
who had better not. I have a friend in another state who, when I am
there, asks me to play golf with him. I enjoy playing with him, but I
have discovered that he is a man who lacks tact even though he has a
zeal to witness for the Lord. I have seen him make waitresses angry. I
have seen him make strangers that we meet angry. He says to me, "You
know, there is surely a lot of opposition to the Gospel today, isn't
there?" Well, I couldn't help but say to him, "I don't think there is as
much opposition as you think there is. It might have something to do
with the way you present the Gospel."

Then I called his attention to the way the Lord Jesus witnessed to
the woman at the well. One of the most hostile persons that the Lord
Jesus ever approached was that Samaritan woman who came down to
the well. She was defiant. Have you ever noticed how He approached
her? He didn't approach her as if He had something to cram down her
throat. He asked her for a drink of water. He took the lowly place by
asking her for something. Then He very courteously said, "Oh, I could
have given you living water if you had asked for it." Finally she did ask
for it, but He didn't offer it until she asked for it.

Before we attempt to cram the Gospel down the throats of people,
we need to give them a little appetite for it. They should see something
in our lives that will make them *want* to know about the Lord Jesus.

However, it it true that there is an opposition to the Word of God,
and we find it coming sometimes from unexpected quarters.

"The watchmen that went about the city found me, they smote me."
This girl is having a difficult time. She is being hurt by those who
should have been protecting her.

This same situation occurs in Christian circles. Many a preacher in our society finds himself deserted by a board that has turned against him because his preaching bothers their consciences. Many times opposition to the Gospel comes from those who should be protecting it.

Now this girl, the bride, meets the daughters of Jerusalem. Here we find antiphonal singing. The bride sings one part, and the daughters of Jerusalem sing an answering part. This sounds very much like an opera.

The bride says:

> **I charge you, O daughters of Jerusalem, if ye find my beloved, that he tell him, that I am sick of love [Song 5:8].**

"If you find him, tell him how much I miss him. Tell him how much I love him, and let him know that I am looking for him." Her heart is sick and her whole being is yearning after him. The garden has lost its fragrance; the myrrh and frankincense don't mean much to her now; and the beauty of the flowers has withered.

Now in this antiphony the daughters of Jerusalem answer:

> **What is thy beloved more than another beloved, O thou fairest among women? what is thy beloved more than another beloved, that thou dost so charge us? [Song 5:9].**

Their answer sounds rather skeptical. In effect they are saying, "This one that you say means so much to you, why is he more to you than you might expect another to be to us?" "What is thy beloved more than another beloved?" Who is this Jesus anyway? What makes you think Jesus is different from anyone else? There have been other great religious leaders. Why do you think that Jesus is different from them? Why do you think that He is who He claims to be? Jesus was only a man. That is the kind of skepticism we hear.

May I say to you, there has been a lot of discussion about Jesus. There has been more controversy about Him than any person who has ever lived. He is the most controversial figure in history. Let me ask you a question. If someone today tried to show that Julius Caesar was a real rascal, would you get all excited about it and rise to his defense? If someone tried to show that Julius Caesar was a saint, would you be all excited about that and try to argue about it? It wouldn't excite me. I'd let anyone think whatever he wanted to think about Julius Caesar. I wouldn't argue with him. But the minute you mention Jesus Christ, the whole human family chooses sides. It is interesting that God forces us to make a decision about His Son. He wouldn't let Pilate off without making a decision. Pilate tried to evade any involvement. He called for a basin of water and washed his hands, saying, ". . . I am innocent of the blood of this just person . . ." (Matt. 27:24). How wrong he was! The oldest creed of the church, which has been recited for over nineteen hundred years by multitudes of people, includes these words: "Crucified under Pontius Pilate." Pontius Pilate, you didn't wash your hands; you made a decision. God forced you to make a decision. Pilate thought that he was the judge and that Jesus was the prisoner. He didn't realize that Christ was the judge and he was the prisoner. And still in our contemporary society every man must make a decision.

"What is thy beloved more than another beloved?" In anthologies of religion, great religious leaders are listed who are called founders of religions: Moses, Jesus, Mohammed, Ghandi, Buddha, and all the rest. According to Tertullian, the early church father, the Christians in the early church would rather have died than have Jesus put down on a place with the heathen deities of the Roman Empire. They refused to even take a pinch of incense and place it before the image of Caesar. They wouldn't do it, because their Beloved was different; He was *God*.

## THE BEAUTY OF THE BELOVED

Now the bride is going to answer. She is going to respond to their skepticism. You would think that they had her cooled off and that she would tone down what she says about the bridegroom. But it didn't work that way. Actually, she now waxes eloquent concerning him.

**My beloved is white and ruddy, the chiefest among ten thousand.**

His head is as the most fine gold, his locks are bushy, and black as a raven.

His eyes are as the eyes of doves by the rivers of waters, washed with milk, and fitly set.

His cheeks are as a bed of spices, as sweet flowers: his lips like lilies, dropping sweet smelling myrrh.

His hands are as gold rings set with the beryl: his belly is as bright ivory overlaid with sapphires.

His legs are as pillars of marble, set upon sockets of fine gold: his countenance is as Lebanon, excellent as the cedars.

His mouth is most sweet: yea, he is all together lovely. This is my beloved, and this is my friend, O daughters of Jerusalem [Song 5:10-16].

There is something here that is very obvious, and that is that she describes him in minute detail. Do you know what that means? It means that she knew him. She knew him intimately.

My friend, if you are going to defend the Lord Jesus Christ today, if you are going to witness for Him, you must know Him. Not only do you need to know who He is, but you need to know Him enough to be able to wax eloquent on His behalf. When I say be eloquent, I don't necessarily mean eloquent in language. I mean full of enthusiasm, excitement, love, and zeal for His person. You and I need not only to know Him, but we must *love* Him. That is the challenge that we find here. The bride knew Him. She knew Him and she loved Him. She says that He is the chiefest among ten thousand.

Many people have written about the person of Christ because He is altogether lovely even in His humanity. Dr. C. I. Scofield, the man who wrote the first notes for *The Scofield Reference Bible*, wrote about the Lord Jesus in a tract entitled, "The Loveliness of Jesus." Let me share part of it with you:

All other greatness has been marred by littleness, all other wisdom has been flawed by folly, all other goodness has been tainted by imperfection; Jesus Christ remains the only Being of whom, without gross flattery, it could be asserted, "He is altogether lovely."

My theme, then, is: The Loveliness of Christ.

First of all, as it seems to me, this loveliness of Christ consists in His perfect humanity. Am I understood? I do not now mean that He was a perfect human, but that He was perfectly human.

In everything but our sins, and our evil natures, He is one with us. He grew in stature and in grace. He labored, and wept, and prayed, and loved. He was tempted in all points as we are—sin apart. With Thomas, we confess Him Lord and God; we adore and revere Him, but beloved, there is no other who establishes with us such intimacy, who comes so close to these human hearts of ours; no one in the universe of whom we are so little afraid. He enters as simply and naturally into our twentieth century lives as if He had been reared in the same street. He is not one of the ancients. How wholesomely and genuinely human He is! Martha scolds Him; John, who has seen Him raise the dead, still the tempest and talk with Moses and Elijah on the mount, does not hesitate to make a pillow of His breast at supper. Peter will not let Him wash his feet, but afterwards wants his head and hands included in the ablution. They ask Him foolish questions, and rebuke Him, and venerate and adore Him all in a breath; and He calls them by their first names, and tells them to fear not, and assures them of His love. And in all this He seems to me altogether lovely.

He is altogether lovely. Now the important question is this: Is He altogether lovely to you? Are you able to speak of Him with the enthusiasm the bride had for her bridegroom? We must know Christ intimately if we are to witness of Him. And we must love Him. When one comes to Christ it is not a business transaction. He is wonderful, and I do not think that we laud Him, glorify Him, lift Him up, worship Him, and bow before Him with thanksgiving enough. He is wonderful any way that you look at Him.

Let me quote again from Dr. Scofield's essay:

The saintliness of Jesus is so warm and human that it attracts and inspires. We find in it nothing austere and inaccessible, like a statue in a niche. The beauty of His holiness reminds one rather of a rose, or a bank of violets.

Jesus receives sinners and eats with them—all kinds of sinners. Nicodemus, the moral, religious sinner, and Mary of Magdala, "out of whom went seven devils"—the shocking kind of sinner. He comes into sinful lives as a bright, clear stream enters a stagnant pool. The stream is not afraid of contamination but its sweet energy cleanses the pool.

I remark again, and as connected with this that His sympathy is altogether lovely.

He is always being "touched with compassion." The multitude without a shepherd, the sorrowing widow of Nain, the little dead child of the ruler, the demoniac of Gadara, the hungry five thousand—what ever suffers touches Jesus. His very wrath against the scribes and Pharisees is but the excess of His sympathy for those who suffer under their hard self-righteousness.

Did you ever find Jesus looking for "deserving poor"? He "healed all their sick." And what grace in His sympathy! Why did He touch that poor leper? He could have healed him with a word as He did the nobleman's son. Why, for years the wretch had been an outcast, cut off from kin, dehumanized. He lost the sense of being a man. It was defilement to approach him. Well, the touch of Jesus made him human again.

A Christian woman, laboring among the moral lepers of London, found a poor street girl desperately ill in a bare, cold room. With her own hands she ministered to her, changing her bed linen, procuring medicines, nourishing food, a fire, and making the poor place as bright and cheery as possible, and then she said, "May I pray with you?"

"No," said the girl, "you don't care for me; you are doing this to get to heaven."

Many days passed with the Christian woman unwearily kind, the sinful girl hard and bitter. At last the Christian said:

"My dear, you are nearly well now, and I shall not come again, but as it is my last visit, I want you to let me kiss you," and the pure lips that had known only prayers and holy words met the lips defiled by oaths and by unholy caresses—and then, my friends, the hard heart broke. That was Christ's way.

As I read this essay from Dr. Scofield, my thoughts turn back to the very beginning of the Song of Solomon in chapter 1, verse 2: "Let him kiss me with the kisses of his mouth: for thy love is better than wine." He wants to bestow His love, His affection, His care, His grace, His mercy upon us today, and we are as hard as that poor sinning girl.

Again, I quote from Dr. Scofield:

Can you fancy Him calling a convention of the Pharisees to discuss methods of reaching the "masses"? That leads me to remark that His humility was altogether lovely, and He, the only one who ever had the choice of how and where He should be born, entered this life as one of the "masses."

What meekness, what lowliness! "I am among you as one that serveth." He "began to wash His disciples' feet." "When He was reviled He reviled not again." "As a sheep before her shearers is dumb, so He openeth not His mouth." Can you think of Jesus posing and demanding His rights?

But it is in His way with sinners that the supreme loveliness of Christ is most sweetly shown. How gentle He is, yet how faithful; how considerate, how respectable. Nicodemus, candid and sincere, but proud of his position as a master in Israel, and timid lest he should imperil it, "comes to Jesus by night." Before he departs "the Master," Nicodemus has learned his utter ignorance of the first step toward the kingdom, and goes away to think over the personal application of "they loved darkness rather than light, because their deeds were evil." But he has not heard one harsh word, one utterance that can wound his self-respect.

When He speaks to that silent despairing woman, after her accusers have gone out, one by one, He uses for "woman" the same word as He used when addressing His mother from the cross.

Follow Him to Jacob's well at high noon and hear His conversation with the woman of Samaria. How patiently He unfolds the deepest truths, how gently, yet faithfully He presses the great ulcer of sin which is eating away her soul. But He could not be more respectable to Mary of Bethany.

Even in the agonies of death He could hear the cry of despairing faith. When conquerors return from far wars in strange lands they bring their chiefest captive as a trophy. It was enough for Christ to take back to heaven the soul of a thief.

Yea, He is altogether lovely. And now I have left myself no room to speak of His dignity, of His virile manliness, of His perfect courage. There is in Jesus a perfect equipoise of various perfections. All the elements of perfect character are in lovely balance. His gentleness is never weak. His courage is never brutal. My friends, you may study these things for yourself. Follow Him through all the scenes of outrage and insult on the night and morning of His arrest and trial. Behold Him before the high priest, before Pilate, before Herod. See Him brow-beaten, bullied, scourged, smitten upon the face, spit upon, mocked. How His inherent greatness comes out. Not once does He lose His self-poise, His high dignity.

Let me ask some unsaved sinner here to follow Him still further. Go with the jeering crowd without the gates; see Him stretched upon the great rough cross and hear the dreadful sound of the sledge as the spikes are forced through His hands and feet. See, as the yelling mob falls back, the cross, bearing this gentlest, sweetest, bravest, loveliest man, upreared until it falls into the socket in the rock. "And sitting down, they watched Him there." You watch, too. Hear Him ask the Father to forgive His murderers, hear all the cries from the cross. Is He not altogether lovely? What does it all mean?

"He bore our sins in His own body on the tree."

"By Him all that believe are justified from all things."

"Verily, verily, I say unto you, he that believeth on Me hath everlasting life."

I close with a word of personal testimony. This is my beloved, and this is my friend. Will you not accept Him as your Savior, and beloved and friend?

That is the end of the quotation, and I want to add my own "Amen" to it. That means I agree with every word of it. My Beloved is the chiefest among ten thousand. He is the One who is altogether lovely.

Was it merely the son of Joseph and Mary who crossed the world's horizon more that nineteen hundred years ago? Was it merely human blood that was spilled on Calvary's hill for the redemption of sinners? What thinking man can keep from exclaiming, "My Lord and my God"?

"This is my beloved, and this is my friend, O daughters of Jerusalem" (v. 16). She knew Him. She loved Him. She makes Him known.

# CHAPTER 6

## FROM SKEPTICS TO BELIEVERS

**Whither is thy beloved gone, O thou fairest among woman? whither is thy beloved turned aside? that we may seek him with thee [Song 6:1].**

The daughters of Jerusalem are not so skeptical and cynical now. They are willing to go with the bride to help her find him. They want to see this one whom the bride has told them about. They conclude that he must be wonderful, and they want to see him for themselves.

The Bible tells us that whoever seeks will find. The Lord Jesus has said that if anyone would come to Him, He would in no wise cast him out.

**My beloved is gone down into his garden, to the beds of spices, to feed in the gardens, and to gather lilies.**

**I am my beloved's, and my beloved is mine: he feedeth among the lilies [Song 6:2–3].**

She has located the bridegroom. What assurance, what satisfaction, what joy she has!

God is satisfied with Jesus. He has said, ". . . This is my beloved Son: hear him" (Luke 9:35). He is satisfied with the work which Christ accomplished for us on the cross. He says that if we will come to His Son, we will not perish but have everlasting life. What an invitation has gone out!

## THE KING'S DELIGHT IN THE BRIDE

**Thou art beautiful, O my love, as Tirzah, comely as Jerusalem, terrible as an army with banners.**

Turn away thine eyes from me, for they have overcome me: thy hair is as a flock of goats that appear from Gilead.

Thy teeth are as a flock of sheep which go up from the washing, whereof every one beareth twins, and there is not one barren among them.

As a piece of a pomegranate are thy temples within thy locks.

There are threescore queens, and fourscore concubines, and virgins without number.

My dove, my undefiled is but one; she is the only one of her mother, she is the choice one of her that bare her. The daughters saw her, and blessed her; yea, the queens and the concubines, and they praised her [Song 6:4–9].

"Thou art beautiful, O my love, as Tirzah"—the beautiful expressions throughout this section are the bridegroom's response to the long, intense, sorrowful, and patient search for his presence. A. Moody Stuart gives us this helpful background: "Tirzah was the royal city of one of the ancient kings of Canaan, and afterwards for a time of the kings of Israel. The word signifies pleasant, and the situation of the city, as well as the town itself, was probably remarkable for beauty. . . .'Beautiful as Tirzah'—how gracious the address to the slothful, sorrowing, smitten Bride! but 'whom he loveth he loveth unto the end,' though we change, He is 'the same yesterday, to-day, and for ever.'"

> Who is she that looketh forth as the morning, fair as the moon, clear as the sun, and terrible as an army with banners? [Song 6:10].

This shows us how the Lord views the Rapture of the church. It is natural that we look at the Rapture from the viewpoint of our expectations. "For the Lord himself shall descend from heaven with a shout, with the voice of the archangel, and with the trump of God: and the dead in Christ shall rise first" (1 Thess. 4:16). But the Lord looks at it from His side. He will be calling His own. When the church comes into His presence, the angelic hosts will see one of the greatest sights that will be beheld in all of eternity. This will be the most thrilling event for us and for Him too. Then they will say about the church, "Who is she that looketh forth as the morning, fair as the moon, clear as the sun, and terrible as an army with banners?" This same union of Christ and the church is pictured for us in the lives of Isaac and Rebekah. Isaac was walking in the field when he looked up and saw the caravan of camels coming. Rebekah was on one of the camels in that caravan. She got off the camel and came to meet her bridegroom. What a glorious picture of the time when you and I will go into the presence of the Lord Jesus.

## THE RESPONSE OF THE BRIDE

**I went down into the garden of nuts to see the fruits of the valley, and to see whether the vine flourished, and the pomegranates budded.**

**Or ever I was aware, my soul made me like the chariots of Amminadib [Song 6:11–12].**

I just can't resist intruding here with a little anecdote. A friend of mine who is a preacher went to speak to a group of unbelievers. They were a group that included college professors. Many of their theories were way out in left field. They really understood very little about the real issues of life. I asked my friend, "What do you think you accomplished by going to that group?" He answered, "I don't know that I accomplished very much, but I was certainly scriptural. I went down into the garden of nuts." There's no question about that!

Seriously, the bride had something very different in mind. It is interesting that this is the third garden we see in the Song of Solomon. A. Moody Stuart calls our attention to this: "The first garden is in spring, full of flowers and tender grapes with nothing mature; the second garden is in autumn, full of spices and ripe fruits with nothing imperfect; and this third garden is in the end of winter, but with the immediate prospect of a new spring. . . . It is still winter, but the winter is on the very point of bursting in a new spring, and the Bride descends into the garden of nuts to watch the first sproutings of the valley, the earliest blossoming of the vine, and the budding of the pomegranate."

Stuart compares this to the experience of the disciples of our Lord after His ascension as they wait in Jerusalem for the promise of the Father. In a sense they go into the garden to watch for a fresh outbreak of a new spring. The entire Old Testament is a new treasure to them since Jesus had ". . . expounded unto them in all the scriptures the things concerning himself" (Luke 24:27). While gathering and breaking open those old treasures of the past, the Spirit came in an unexpected manner and with unexpected power, which could not be described more exactly than in the words of the Song, "or ever I was aware, my soul made me like the chariots of Amminadib."

My friend, the Word of God is a garden, a whole garden of unopened nuts. There are innumerable kernels in the Word of God waiting to be opened and enjoyed by the bride of Christ.

> **Return, return, O Shulamite; return, return, that we may look upon thee. What will ye see in the Shulamite? As it were the company of two armies [Song 6:13].**

The statement is made that the bride of Christ will be for the demonstration of God's grace throughout the ages: "That in the ages to come he might shew the exceeding riches of his grace in his kindness toward us through Christ Jesus" (Eph. 2:7). All of the created universe is going to see us. None of us is worthy to be there, but we are going to be there because we are in Christ. It is because He loved us and gave Himself for us. We will be there for His glory and for our good. I can't think of anything better than that!

# CHAPTERS 7 AND 8

## PORTRAIT OF THE BRIDE

In the first nine verses of chapter 7 the bridegroom tells of his delight in his bride, using one beautiful figure after another. Harry A. Ironside makes this comment: "It is a wonderful thing to know that the Lord has far more delight in His people than we ourselves have ever had in Him. Some day we shall enjoy Him to the fullest; some day He will be everything to us; but as long as we are here, we never appreciate Him as much as He appreciates us. But as she listens to his expression of love, her heart is assured; she has the sense of restoration and fellowship."

## SATISFACTION OF THE BRIDE

She says all she needs to say about her beloved in one verse:

**I am my beloved's, and his desire is toward me [Song 7:10].**

Twice before we have heard the bride say, "My beloved is mine, and I am his," but A. Moody Stuart draws our attention to the fact that this is an expression of far greater fullness. Although it implies the outgoing of desire from the heart of Christ, it expressly declares what is much more precious: that the *believer* knows the strength of Christ's desire toward him. Stuart puts it this way: "'I know', saith the Lord, 'the thoughts that I think towards you, thoughts of good and not of evil'; the Lord who thinks them knows them, but he toward whom they are thought is often ignorant, or doubtful, or unbelieving regarding them; and most blessed are the souls that can respond, 'We have known and believed the love that God hath to us.'" *We* are objects of *His* desire— what wondrous grace!

## THE VERY BROTHER

**O that thou wert as my brother, that sucked the breasts of my mother! when I should find thee without, I would kiss thee; yea, I should not be despised [Song 8:1].**

"My brother, that sucked the breast of my mother" refers, of course, to a brother born of the same mother, implying the nearest possible relationship. It is this kind of a brother the Lord Jesus has become to us—"For verily he took not on him the nature of angels; but he took on him the seed of Abraham" (Heb. 2:16), becoming flesh of our flesh and bone of our bone.

"I would kiss thee; yea, I should not be despised." A great many true believers are afraid or ashamed to openly confess that they love Christ. Oh, my friend, don't *say* you love Him if you don't, but if your life reveals that you do love Him, folk will not despise you for speaking of it.

**I would lead thee, and bring thee into my mother's house, who would instruct me: I would cause thee to drink of spiced wine of the juice of my pomegranate [Song 8:2].**

"I would cause thee to drink of spiced wine of the juice of my pomegranate." Stuart has well said, "It is our part to give Christ the best entertainment in our power, to spare nothing on him, to gather all of him and present all to him, that is choicest and best. But the full reference of these words is to the final 'marriage of the Lamb when his wife shall have made herself ready,' and when Christ 'shall drink the fruit of the vine new with her in his Father's kingdom.'"

## THE RELYING WEAKNESS OF LOVE

**Who is this that cometh up from the wilderness, leaning upon her beloved? I raised thee up under the apple tree:**

**there thy mother brought thee forth: there she brought thee forth that bare thee [Song 8:5].**

"Leaning upon her beloved." The final stage of the true believer's life is characterized by weakness, by dependence, and by love. In youth we ". . . mount[ed] up with wings as eagles . . ." (Isa. 40:31) when His banner over us was love. In manhood we ran without being wearied—even when (as Stuart says) we sought Him sorrowing through the streets of Jerusalem—but in our declining years we are more apt to lean heavily upon Him in childlike trust. And when we finally recognize our utter dependence upon Christ and the truth of His statement that without Him we can do *nothing*, then He can use our service.

**Set me as a seal upon thine heart, as a seal upon thine arm: for love is strong as death; jealousy is cruel as the grave: the coals thereof are coals of fire, which hath a most vehement flame [Song 8:6].**

"For love is strong as death." Death, with all its terrors, was the price of the love of the Lord Jesus Christ to lost men, but it did not deter Him—He loved us and gave Himself for us, enduring the cross and despising the shame. Also death has been ten thousand times before the bride of the slain Lamb, and she ". . . loved not [her life] . . . unto the death" (Rev. 12:11); for ". . . neither death, nor life . . . shall be able to separate us from the love of God, which is in Christ Jesus our Lord" (Rom. 8:38–39).

"Jealousy is cruel as the grave"—the all devouring grave knows no pity. Stuart reminds us that it was jealousy cruel as the grave that moved Elijah, who was very jealous for the Lord God of hosts, to slay the prophets of Baal at the brook Kishon and let not one escape. And "it was jealousy that stirred Paul to utter the righteous and holy, yet tremendous curse—'if any man love not the Lord Jesus Christ, let him be Anathema Maranatha.' This jealousy, with its grave-like cruelty, our protesting and suffering forefathers knew better than we; and it produced a remarkable but noble mingling of ardent love to Jesus with tenderness of conscience and manly boldness, which made little account either of their lives or those of others, when placed in competition with the honour of the Lord Jesus Christ."

"The coals thereof are coals of fire." This reminds us of the love that burned in the heart of the Lord Jesus Christ when He said, ". . . The zeal of thine house hath eaten me up" (John 2:17). Stuart adds: "Ascending to the right hand of the Father, he kindled within the hearts of his disciples the same divine fire that burned within himself; sending down the Holy Ghost to rest upon them as flames or tongues of fire: and the fire of love burned more mightily within them, than the visible flames that encircled their heads."

> Many waters cannot quench love, neither can the floods
> drown it: if a man would give all the substance of his
> house for love, it would utterly be contemned [Song 8:7].

"Many waters cannot quench love." Oh, how many times we have failed Him; yet our repeated failures have not quenched His love, nor has it been drowned by the floods of our sins.

"If a man would give all the substance of his house for love, it would utterly be contemned." The word *contemned* means to be loathed, despised. God is not asking for our money or our service; He is asking for our *love*. If we don't love Him, He *despises* the so-called Christian work we try to do and the money we put in the offering plate.

## THE LITTLE SISTER

> We have a little sister, and she hath no breasts: what
> shall we do for our sister in the day when she shall be
> spoken for? [Song 8:8].

The "little sister" is, many Bible teachers feel, symbolic of the church of the Gentiles. "What shall we do for our sister?" was the thorny question in the early church. Acts 15 records the Council at Jerusalem which was convened to resolve the conflict between the Gentile converts and the Hebrew converts who had no intention of giving up the Mosaic system.

"In the day when she shall be spoken for." Well, who would speak for her? Nobody would want her. Gentiles were outcasts. But the day came when this sister was spoken for by the great Bridegroom of the church who called her to Himself. My friend, He did not choose us because we were attractive, but because He saw our lost condition and loved us.

Now that the "little sister" is accepted by Christ, what kind of reception will she get from the elder sister?

> **If she be a wall, we will build upon her a palace of silver: and if she be a door, we will enclose her with boards of cedar [Song 8:9].**

"If she be a wall, we will build upon her a palace of silver." Since the Gentiles were being accepted by God, they were being ". . . builded together [with the Hebrew Christians] for an habitation of God through the Spirit" (Eph. 2:22). The Jewish church faced the question: what should be built on it? Circumcision, ceremonies, different rites and ordinances—yokes which neither the Hebrew fathers nor children were able to bear? James expressed the feeling of the elder sister: ". . . my sentence is, that we trouble not them, which from among the Gentiles are turned to God" (Acts 15:19). The council agreed not to force Gentile believers into the Mosaic system, but to accept them as they were and do everything possible to build them up in the faith.

> **I am a wall, and my breasts like towers: then was I in his eyes as one that found favour [Song 8:10].**

This is the rejoicing of the "little sister." When the gentile church received the good news of the council's decision, ". . . they rejoiced for the consolation" (Acts 15:31). Recognized now as a wall in God's temple, they greatly rejoiced in the privilege. "Now therefore ye are no more strangers and foreigners, but fellow citizens with the saints, and of the household of God; And are built upon the foundation of the apostles and prophets, Jesus Christ himself being the chief corner stone; In whom all the building fitly framed together groweth unto an holy temple in the Lord: In whom ye also are builded together for an habitation of God through the Spirit" (Eph. 2:19–22).

"My breasts like towers"—the little sister, symbolic of the gentile church, soon nourished many sons and daughters with the sincere milk of the Word. The Gentile church grew with amazing rapidity so that the little sister now has become both more beautiful and more honored than the elder.

There is a missionary message in this parable of the little sister. You and I need to recognize that the little sister included all nations in our day. In many parts of the world there are folk who have never responded to the call of the Bridegroom simply because they have not heard His voice. And ". . . how shall they hear without a preacher?" (Rom. 10:14).

## THE TRANSFER OF THE VINEYARD

**Solomon had a vineyard at Baalhamon; he let out the vineyard unto keepers; every one for the fruit thereof was to bring a thousand pieces of silver [Song 8:11].**

"Solomon had a vineyard." Solomon is symbolic of Christ. The bride, which is the united church of Jews and Gentiles, tells the story of the vineyard. First it was under the charge of its original keepers, the nation of Israel, and next it was committed to her own care. It is the same parable that Jesus told in Matthew 21:33–46 about a certain householder who planted a vineyard, put a wall around it, dug a winepress in it, and built a tower, then rented it out to vinegrowers while he went on a long journey. At harvest time he sent his servants to receive the produce, and they were beaten or killed. Finally he sent his own son. "But when the husbandmen saw the son, they said among themselves, This is the heir; come, let us kill him, and let us seize on his inheritance. And they caught him, and cast him out of the vineyard, and slew him. When the lord therefore of the vineyard cometh, what will he do unto these husbandmen?" (Matt. 21:38–40). The answer is that he will come and destroy the husbandmen and will give the vineyard to others.

> **My vineyard, which is mine, is before me: thou, O Solomon, must have a thousand, and those that keep the fruit thereof two hundred [Song 8:12].**

"Those that keep the fruit thereof two hundred"—they are to be paid for their work. "Even so hath the Lord ordained that they which preach the gospel should live of the gospel" (1 Cor. 9:14).

"Thou, O Solomon, must have a thousand," promising, unlike her predecessor, that full revenue shall be the Lord's; yet she tends it with her whole heart as if it were her own—"my vineyard, which is mine, is before me."

Historically the early church kept the vineyard just that way. But, unfortunately, the church in our day presents a different picture. Oh that you and I, as members of the bride of Christ, will be faithful in the portion of the vineyard God has allotted to our care!

> **Make haste, my beloved, and be thou like to a roe or to a young hart upon the mountains of spices [Song 8:14].**

The bride is saying to the Lord of the vineyard, "Return!" Over in the Book of Revelation the last thing she says is, ". . . Even so, come, Lord Jesus" (Rev. 22:20).

My friend, I don't believe you can honestly say that unless you *know* Him, unless you *love* Him, and unless you *make Him known*. Can you look up and say, "Come, Lord Jesus, I want you to come"? Paul said that God will give a crown to those who *love* His appearing. And to love His appearing means to love Him—even as a bride eagerly anticipates and prepares for the coming of the bridegroom, her beloved.

Let us conclude this marvelous Song of Solomon with the lines of Herbert:

Come, Lord, my head doth burn, my heart is sick,
While thou dost ever, ever stay:
Thy long deferrings wound me to the quick,
My spirit gaspeth night and day.
O show thyself to me,
Or take me up to thee!

Yet if thou stayest still, why must I stay?
My God, what is this world to me?
This world of woe? hence all ye clouds, away!
Away! I must get up and see.
O show thyself to me,
Or take me up to thee!

We talk of harvest; there are no such things,
But when we leave our corn and hay.
There is no fruitful year, but that which brings
The last and loved, though dreadful, day
O show thyself to me,
Or take me up to thee!

# BIBLIOGRAPHY
## (Recommended for Further Study)

Darby, J. N. *Synopsis of the Books of the Bible*. Addison, Illinois: Bible Truth Publishers.

Gaebelein, Arno C. *The Annotated Bible*. 1917. Reprint. Neptune, New Jersey: Loizeaux Brothers, 1971.

Glickman, S. Craig. *A Song for Lovers*. Downers Grove, Illinois: Inter-Varsity Press, 1976. (A fine treatment of Song of Solomon)

Gray, James M. *Commentary on the Whole Bible*. Old Tappan, New Jersey: Fleming H. Revell Co., 1906.

Hadley, E. C. *The Song of Solomon*. Sunbury, Pennsylvania: Believer's Bookshelf, n.d.

Ironside, H. A. *Addresses on the Song of Solomon*. Neptune, New Jersey: Loizeaux Brothers, 1933. (An excellent treatment)

Jensen, Irving L. *Ecclesiastes and the Song of Solomon*. Chicago, Illinois: Moody Press, 1974. (A self-study guide)

Kelly, William. *Lectures on the Song of Solomon*. Addison, Illinois: Bible Truth Publishers, n.d.

Miller, Andrew. *The Song of Solomon*. Addison, Illinois: Bible Truth Publishers, n.d.

Unger, Merrill F. *Unger's Bible Handbook*. Chicago, Illinois: Moody Press, 1966.

Unger, Merrill F. *Unger's Commentary on the Old Testament*. Vol. I. Chicago, Illinois: Moody Press, 1981.